Bering Sea

NORTH ASIA

CENTRAL
ASIA

NORTH
PACIFIC
OCEAN

SOUTHEAST
ASIA

Equator

INDIAN
OCEAN

AUSTRALASIA
& OCEANIA

Tasman
Sea

SOUTHERN
OCEAN

LONELY PLANET'S

BEST IN TRAVEL

2012

THE BEST TRENDS, DESTINATIONS, JOURNEYS & EXPERIENCES FOR THE UPCOMING YEAR

MELBOURNE ⊙ OAKLAND ⊙ LONDON

BUDDHIST MONKS WILL BLOW YOU AWAY WITH HORNS AND CONCH SHELLS AT THE TAMSHING MONASTERY, TSECHU

CONTENTS

GAVIN GOUGH » LPI

FOREWORD

WELCOME TO 2012. IT'S GOING TO BE A CRACKER, AND YOU HOLD THE REASONS WHY IN YOUR HANDS – 10 COUNTRIES, 10 REGIONS AND 10 CITIES THAT OFFER THE VERY BEST IN TRAVEL FOR 2012, PLUS TOPICAL TRAVEL LISTS SPANNING THE GLOBE.

Best in Travel starts with hundreds of ideas from everyone at Lonely Planet, including our extended family of travellers, bloggers and tweeters. Once we're confident we have the cream of 2012's travel choices, the final selection is made by a panel of in-house travel experts, based on topicality, excitement, value and that special X-factor. As with last year, our top 10 countries, regions and cities are ranked in order. Our picks tend to generate plenty of debate, and we're looking forward to hearing what readers think of the selections.

Where came out on top? It's no surprise that London, celebrating its Olympic year, is the essential city. Uganda, a rising adventure sports and wildlife-spotting destination, claimed the top country spot. Coastal Wales, beautiful and wild, is the pick of regions around the world.

Everywhere we've chosen has something special to mark it out for this year. Canada's Maritime Provinces stand out in 2012 due to their links with the *Titanic* centenary, and the impact this short-lived vessel had on other locations is noted on p196. Others have a buzz about them that we picked up on the road and couldn't keep to ourselves: step forward Croatia's Hvar Island, Stockholm and Santiago de Chile. And some places are

worth visiting before the crowds get there – we're looking at you, Darwin and Bhutan.

If you want to know what the travel trends are for 2012 then look no further. As you might expect, the hottest topics are included in our Best Things to Do in 2012. We bring you best places to Glamp (combining glamour and camping), Sleep with Celebrities and find some Intrepid Romance. And, as everyone's looking to get the most bang for their buck, our list of Best-Value Destinations is also recommended reading.

One other thing: in choosing countries, we aren't sticking to the formal definition but rather including places that travellers experience as a distinct destination. New Caledonia is a territory of France, and Taiwan is not recognised by the United Nations, but we've included them as 'countries' because they are culturally and geographically separate identities.

Whether you're planning on watching football in Ukraine, avoiding the Apocalypse on the Ruta Maya or finding surprises in cities like Orlando or Bengaluru, you'll find everything you need for 2012 right here. All you need to do now, as a wise man once said, is go.

Tom Hall, Lonely Planet Travel Editor

010
UGANDA

014
MYANMAR
(BURMA)

018
UKRAINE

022
JORDAN

026
DENMARK

LONELY PLANET'S
TOP 10 COUNTRIES

030
BHUTAN

034
CUBA

038
NEW CALEDONIA

042
TAIWAN

046
SWITZERLAND

'…explorers in search of the source of the Nile won't leave disappointed. Just make sure you discover it before everyone else does.'

by Oliver Smith

01 UGANDA

- ✪ **POPULATION** 34.6 MILLION
- ✪ **FOREIGN VISITORS PER YEAR** 800,000
- ✪ **CAPITAL** KAMPALA
- ✪ **LANGUAGES** ENGLISH, SWAHILI
- ✪ **MAJOR INDUSTRY** AGRICULTURE
- ✪ **UNIT OF CURRENCY** UGANDAN SHILLING (UGX)
- ✪ **COST INDEX** BOTTLE OF NILE SPECIAL BEER UGX 2500 (US$1), SHORT BODA-BODA (MOTORBIKE TAXI) RIDE UGX 5000 (US$2), DORM ROOM UGX 12,000 (US$5), GORILLA-TRACKING PERMIT PER DAY UGX 1 MILLION (US$500)

WHY GO IN 2012? THE FUTURE IS NOW

Uganda is the Cinderella of East Africa. While (not-so-ugly) sisters Tanzania and Kenya became big-name safari destinations, attracting visitors from around the world, Uganda's invitation to the party somehow got lost in the post.

It's taken nasty dictatorships and a brutal civil war to keep Uganda off the tourist radar, but stability is returning and it won't be long before visitors come flocking back. After all, this is the source of the river Nile – that mythical place explorers sought since Roman times. It's also where savannah meets the vast lakes of East Africa, and where snow-capped mountains bear down on sprawling jungles. No wonder Winston Churchill called Uganda 'The Pearl of Africa'.

Not so long ago, the tyrannical dictator and 'Last King of Scotland' Idi Amin helped hunt Uganda's big game to the brink of extinction, but today the wildlife is returning with a vengeance. With a bit of luck you will find all the A-listers of the African wilderness – lion, leopard, elephant, hippo, gorilla and chimp – but for now you won't spot busloads of gawping tourists. Murchison Falls National Park is emphatically open for business after years of unrest in northern Uganda, while other national parks have promised to scrub up and unveil new accommodation for 2012. This year Uganda also celebrates the 50th anniversary of its independence; Kampala, one of Africa's safest capital cities, is bound to see off the event with a bang. Still, Uganda still isn't without its problems. Human rights abuses aren't uncommon, and the country breathes a collective sigh whenever President Museveni thinks of another ruse to stay in power for a few more years. But now, as ever, explorers in search of the source of the Nile won't leave disappointed. Just make sure you discover it before everyone else does.

NO SUCH THING AS MONDAYITIS ON THIS WORK COMMUTE

4CORNERS IMAGES » LPI

LIFE-CHANGING EXPERIENCES

Even for the most experienced adventurers in Africa, Uganda is likely to challenge expectations. Scanning the horizon from a hammock in the tropical Ssese Islands, you'll probably have to remind yourself you're in the middle of a vast inland lake. And while hiking the frosty heights of the Ruwenzori mountains, you'll probably forget you're in Africa at all.

Uganda certainly isn't short of superlative thrills, from white-water rafting the Nile to partying hard in Kampala. But it's encounters with nature that are the defining experience of this country – none more so than coming face to face with a silverback gorilla in the Bwindi Impenetrable Forest.

FESTIVALS & EVENTS

✪ In September, the Bayimba International Festival of the Arts brings Ugandan and international performers to Kampala's National Theatre, from hip-hop groups to theatre companies. The Bayimba Foundation also runs events throughout the year in regional Ugandan cities, such as Mbarara, Jinja and Mbale.

ARIADNE VAN ZANDBERGEN » LPI

✪ Uganda celebrates 50 years of independence from the British Empire on 9 October 2012. Plans are currently rather hazy, but it's a certain bet that there'll be celebrations in Kampala and throughout the country.

HOT TOPIC OF THE DAY

A few years ago, it looked like Uganda had won the geological lottery. The discovery of a gigantic oil field beneath Lake Albert sparked dreams of Uganda becoming the Abu Dhabi of East Africa. Following dodgy handshakes in locked rooms, many Ugandans are sceptical that they'll see any benefit. This year oil production is set to begin in earnest, although whether oil will be a blessing or a curse for the country remains to be seen.

MOST BIZARRE SIGHT

The shoebill is the creature on every birder's wish list, partly because it's quite rare but mostly because of its utterly bizarre appearance. Mock at it at your peril though – although it may look like a stork with a shoe attached to its face, the shoebill is a serious bird that eats baby crocodiles for breakfast. It's best observed at Murchison Falls National Park.

◆ MYANMAR (BURMA)

'Rudyard Kipling said Burma is "quite unlike any land you know about" – and that's selling it short.'

by Robert Reid

02 MYANMAR (BURMA)

- ✪ **POPULATION** 54 MILLION
- ✪ **FOREIGN VISITORS PER YEAR** 300,000
- ✪ **CAPITAL** NAYPYIDAW
- ✪ **LANGUAGE:** BURMESE (OFFICIAL), PLUS 106 OTHERS
- ✪ **MAJOR INDUSTRIES:** OIL, NATURAL GAS
- ✪ **UNIT OF CURRENCY:** BURMESE KYAT (K)
- ✪ **COST INDEX:** CUP OF TEA K300 (US$0.25), DOUBLE GUESTHOUSE ROOM K14,400-24,000 (US$12-20), PASS TO BAGAN ARCHAEOLOGICAL ZONE K12,000 (US$10), DAILY BIKE RENTAL K1500-2000 (US$1.25-1.65)

KIMBERLEY COOLE » LPI

WHY GO IN 2012? A WARM WELCOME

'We want people to come to Burma.' That's the words of the National League for Democracy (NLD), the opposition party that has urged foreigners to stay away since 1996. This changed in late 2010, when the NLD revised its boycott to encourage independent travel (as opposed to package tours) following the release of Aung San Suu Kyi, who had spent 15 of the past 20 years under house arrest. As a result, Myanmar is set to be a hot new destination for independent travellers.

Of course, there's never been any doubt about how thrilling a visit to Myanmar can be. Rimmed by mountains and white-sand beaches, the kite-shaped country's most accessible area is the centre, which is filled with timeless towns and countless pagodas, especially the 4000 examples found on Bagan's 26-sq-km riverside plain. Beyond the attractions, there's the fervently Buddhist locals, who might just be the world's sweetest people. The slower pace of life here is reflected in long, low-key conversations, usually over tea, where you'll find yourself good-naturedly referred to as 'brother' or 'sister'.

If you do go, be aware that the revised boycott doesn't mean troubles are over. Despite Suu Kyi's release, at least 2000 other political prisoners remain in jail, and conflicts continue between the military dictatorship and ethnic minorities in the mountainous border zones.

LIFE-CHANGING EXPERIENCES

Rudyard Kipling said Burma is 'quite unlike any land you know about' – and that's selling it short. Watch for splattered pools of spat betel juice, men in skirtlike *longyi* and women decking their cheeks in *thanakha* bark paste. But the best place to soak up the local scene is the teashops (the only thing to outnumber stupas). For about K300, you get tea, the option of light snacks and a licence to sit and chat for hours.

FESTIVALS & EVENTS

✪ Shwedagon Festival, the largest *paya pwe* (pagoda festival) in the country, is held at the 2000-year-old, world-famous Shwedagon pagoda in Yangon on the last full moon before the April new year.

✪ In mid-April, the nationwide three-day Thingyan Festival starts the Myanmar New Year with a serious splash, with buckets of water (or streams shot from hoses) dousing passers-by. It's nicely timed for the height of the dry and hot season.

✪ In October or November, Taunggyi hosts the huge fire-balloon festival, a remarkable scene that anchors Tazaungmon (the eighth month of the Burmese lunar calendar).

RECENT FAD

Fads, sadly enough, rarely trickle down to a people who are happy to have electricity a few hours a day. For those lucky enough to have some money, a 'fad' is a trip to Singapore, a mobile phone or perhaps the ability to start a private business.

WHAT'S HOT...

The internet. BBC radio. Independent travel. Tea.

WHAT'S NOT...

Package tours. Freeing political prisoners.

HOT TOPIC OF THE DAY

Economic sanctions. Debate continues to rage over whether the West should engage with the military dictatorship by loosening sanctions, or leave it to nations that don't impose them (including China, Thailand and India).

RANDOM FACTS

✪ Myanmar or Burma? 'Myanmar' is the government's official name, and sort of the traditional one. 'Burma' is linked to the Bamar majority, and only became the name during the British colonial period.

✪ Locals can find long ways to answer yes/no questions. The local saying is that '1000 words beats 10', so you may find that a simple question like, 'How long have you been a trishaw driver?' will take five minutes to answer – without much clarity either.

FELIX HUG » LPI

'It's through the power of soccer that Ukraine is poised to showcase its charms to unprecedented numbers of visitors.'

by Luke Waterson

03 UKRAINE

- ✪ **POPULATION** 45.7 MILLION

- ✪ **FOREIGN VISITORS PER YEAR** APPROX 20 MILLION

- ✪ **CAPITAL** KIEV

- ✪ **LANGUAGES** UKRAINIAN (OFFICIAL), RUSSIAN, HUNGARIAN, ROMANIAN, POLISH

- ✪ **MAJOR INDUSTRIES** METALS, CHEMICALS, MACHINERY, AGRICULTURE

- ✪ **UNIT OF CURRENCY** UKRAINIAN HRYVNIA (UAH)

- ✪ **COST INDEX** BOTTLE OF OBOLON BEER UAH10 (US$1.25), MIDRANGE DOUBLE HOTEL ROOM UAH600-875 (US$75-110), TAXI RIDE FROM KIEV AIRPORT TO CITY CENTRE UAH200 (US$25), MIDRANGE MEAL IN RESTAURANT UAH150-200 (US$19-25)

ROMAIN CINTRACT © CORBIS

WHY GO IN 2012? THE ADVENTURE KICKS OFF...

It's always the same. When we don't know much about a country, we just fill in the gaps with clichés – and Ukraine, the great unknown of Europe, has had plenty hurled at it. Wide-scale counter-espionage? No, not even in Odessa. Communist grime everywhere you look? One glimpse of glorious Old Town Kiev or the wildlife on unspoilt Crimean shores will set you straight. Wolves? OK, there are wolves, and bears as well if you scour the lovely, lonely Carpathians, but you're more likely to encounter magical folk traditions and Gothic scenery dramatic enough to make Dracula cast an envious eye east. Cheap beer? You bet: it's cheaper than water. Football? Funny you should mention that...

It's through the power of soccer that Ukraine is poised to showcase its charms to unprecedented numbers of visitors. It will co-host Euro 2012 (the European football championships) and the four match venues have been cunningly selected to encourage further travel by visiting football fans. So Lviv becomes the jumping-off point for Carpathian exploration, while Kiev, which stages the final, will become base for forays to the Black Sea coast and, yep, the grim tourist attraction that is Chernobyl. A series of side-trips means the country's hot spots will be easier to access than ever before (good news for those who can't read Cyrillic). When it comes to adventure, Ukraine can definitely go all the way in 2012.

LIFE-CHANGING EXPERIENCES

Kiev caters to pretty diverse tastes: a baroque old town with an 11th-century multi-frescoed cathedral and a 1000-year-old cave monastery, plus the massive 62m-high Motherland monument (no prizes for guessing which regime built that). The drop-dead-gorgeous medieval city of Lviv and the Crimean Peninsula, home to balaclavas and stunning Black Sea scenery, are the other big draws. Don't miss out on the local cuisine: try *borsch* (beetroot broth), *perohy* (dumplings served with potato/cheese), or *kotlety* (fish/mincemeat-stuffed cutlets).

FESTIVALS & EVENTS

✪ Kiev Day, the country's national day, unfolds on the last weekend in May, with a boisterous succession of parades, carnival and fireworks.

✪ Ivana Kupala, the feast of St John the Baptist, is celebrated on the summer solstice (20 June) and has a distinctly pagan feel: wreath-wearing, nature-worshipping and fire-jumping shape the festivities at rural locales country-wide.

✪ Sheshory Festival in July is a three-day celebration of traditional folk music and dance, taking place in the Carpathian village of the same name.

WHAT'S HOT...

Chernobyl. Football.

WHAT'S NOT...

Espionage. Poisoning presidential candidates. *Konjak* (an occasionally-lethal brandy often made with methanol). Praising the Soviet Union.

HOT TOPIC OF THE DAY

The debate on the street is over who should really be in charge. Viktor Yanukovych retook the presidency with less than 50% of the vote in 2011, but should a traditionally eastward-facing politician once accused of election fraud be guiding 21st-century Ukraine? Does it mock the democratic system that Yanukovych's only real rival in the previous campaign was poisoned prior to winning office, then accused of falsifying evidence in his own poisoning? Can the conflicting demands of Ukraine's neighbours to the east and west be reconciled?

MOST BIZARRE SIGHT

Visiting Pripyat: the city built to house Chernobyl plant workers and abandoned following the 1986 explosion due to high radiation levels. Intrepid tour guides have kick-started visits to the ghost town – highlights do include a never-used Ferris wheel and do not include picking plants, which can still carry dangerous doses of radiation. You are fitted with protective clothing and a Geiger counter to monitor your SI blood levels.

'Jordan is an example…of how to modernise while preserving cherished ancient traditions.'

by Oliver Smith

04 JORDAN

POPULATION 6.5 MILLION

FOREIGN VISITORS PER YEAR 4.5 MILLION

CAPITAL AMMAN

LANGUAGE ARABIC

MAJOR INDUSTRIES TOURISM, BANKING, CEMENT

UNIT OF CURRENCY JORDANIAN DINAR (JD)

COST INDEX MIDRANGE HOTEL DOUBLE ROOM JD50 (US$70), DORM ROOM JD10 (US$14), BEDOUIN MAQLOOBEH MEAL JD5 (US$7), TWO-HOUR TAXI RIDE FROM AQABA TO PETRA JD55 (US$77), HORSEBACK RIDE THROUGH THE SIQ AT PETRA JD7 (US$9.80)

TIM BARKER » LPI

WHY GO IN 2012? SHIFTING SANDS

The word is getting out that Jordan is not just about Petra and Indiana Jones. Yes, the ancient 'Red Rose city' is still the jewel in Jordan's crown, but sights such as Wadi Rum, Jerash and Madaba are adding weight to the country's tourism boom. One of the most open, friendly and welcoming nations in the Middle East, Jordan is an example to other states in the region of how to modernise while preserving cherished ancient traditions.

This year marks the 64th birthday of the Hashemite Kingdom of Jordan. A relative baby on the global scene, it was under British control until the end of WWII. Today nobody represents the modern, moderate Jordan better than Queen Rania; one of Earth's most powerful women, she regularly tweets for peace, a valuable commodity in this part of the world. Jordan is a key player thanks to its skills in maintaining good relations with the USA, Israel and the Arab world simultaneously – no mean feat in such a volatile region.

Though poverty is still rife, Jordan's economy is on the up, and its history and tourist infrastructure make it one of the most accessible Arab states for English-speaking travellers. Aside from the established attractions, be sure to check out downtown Amman, with its ultramodern property developments, and Aqaba, which could soon overtake Eilat and Dahab as the top Red Sea desert and diving resort.

LIFE-CHANGING EXPERIENCES

Hike through the psychedelic rock canyons of Wadi Rum, approach Petra on horseback through the Siq and experience the wonder of the candlelit 'Petra by Night' tour. Then time-travel to ancient Rome at the pristine ruins of Jerash, climb up to a crusader castle

GO PSYCHEDELIC WITHOUT ILLEGAL SUBSTANCES AT WADI AL FIDAN GORGE

GIL GIULIO » CORBIS

at Karak or dive to a sunken Lebanese shipwreck in the Red Sea. After the action, enjoy a dish of *maqloobeh* (upside-down chicken and rice) followed by a cup of Bedouin coffee, or get pampered at a luxurious Dead Sea spa resort.

FESTIVALS & EVENTS

✪ Twisting and turning past the spectacular Roman ruins of Jerash before ending at the Dead Sea, the Jordan International Rally in April is always a big thrill for motorsport fans.
✪ Run from Amman to the lowest point on earth in April's Dead Sea Ultra Marathon – the most gruelling of events.
✪ The floodlit Artemis temple sets the backdrop for the Jerash Festival of Art and Culture, showcasing symphony orchestras, ballet and Shakespeare plays in July and August.

RECENT FAD

Wi-fi in the *wadi*. Many hotels in Jordan now have wi-fi connectivity and it's common to see Bedouin tour guides with smartphones and laptops in the middle of the desert.

HOT TOPIC OF THE DAY

Reform not revolution. Since King Abdullah II took the throne in 1999, Jordan has made much economic progress, yet unemployment, oil and food prices remain high. Inspired by other revolutions in the region, the Islamic Action Front (IAF), the political arm of the Muslim Brotherhood, has demanded sweeping reforms. But judging by the posters seen all over the country, the king is still very much revered by Jordanians.

RANDOM FACTS

✪ In 1933 the remains of a 4th century AD church were found at the summit of Jebel Naba (Mt Nebo), where Moses is said to have died.
✪ The Dana Nature Reserve, the most biodiverse area in the country, is home to 703 plant species and is the southernmost area in the world to host the Mediterranean cypress tree.
✪ Wadi Rum provided the widescreen desert backdrop for much of David Lean's 1962 film *Lawrence of Arabia*.
✪ King Abdullah II appeared in *Star Trek: Voyager* in 1996 and toured California on a Harley-Davidson in 2010, but is no longer allowed to sky dive.

MOST BIZARRE SIGHT

Housed inside the Greek Orthodox church of St George is the Madaba Map. Dating from around AD 560, only a quarter of the original mosaic remains, but it includes detailed drawings of the Nile and Jordan rivers, the Dead Sea and Jerusalem – all extraordinarily accurate for its day. Look closely and you'll also see fish, gazelles and, quite randomly, a lion. Intended as a guide for religious pilgrims, these two million tiles were the Google Earth of their day.

DENMARK

EUROPE

NORTH AMERICA

ASIA

AFRICA

'…not only is the living easy in this small, perfectly formed country, but it's also easy on the eye.'

by Sally O'Brien

05 DENMARK

- ✪ **POPULATION** 5.5 MILLION

- ✪ **FOREIGN VISITORS PER YEAR** 4 MILLION

- ✪ **CAPITAL** COPENHAGEN

- ✪ **LANGUAGE** DANISH

- ✪ **MAJOR INDUSTRIES** DESIGN, CLEAN TECH, WIND FARMS, DAIRY, BACON, BEER

- ✪ **UNIT OF CURRENCY** DANISH KRONE (DKK)

- ✪ **COST INDEX** GLASS OF BEER 50DKK (US$9.60), MIDRANGE DOUBLE HOTEL ROOM DKK1000 (US$190), SHORT TAXI RIDE DKK80 (US$15.30), *SMØRREBRØD* 50-100DKK (US$10-19)

WHY GO IN 2012? BETTER LIVING BY DESIGN

Every year, Denmark tops a 'quality of life' list and is revealed as the coolest/happiest/best-looking place on earth, because not only is the living easy in this small, perfectly formed country, but it's also easy on the eye. Viking raids aside, the Danes have long tried to make the world a better place (think generous foreign aid programs and the pursuit of green technology) and they make sure that they lead by example: their homes are stylish recycling-savvy havens of *hygge* (a sense of contented cosiness) and their public spaces are enjoyed by all. And all you have to do is hop on your bike – literally. The flat-as-a-tack capital, Copenhagen, has 390km of cycle lanes and it's hoped that by 2015 some 50% of the city's population will commute to work by bicycle. Country-wide, you'll find around 10,000km of bicycle routes and some four million bikes to share them with, plus you're rarely more than a short pedal from the bracing seaside, the picturesque countryside or an architectural delight, making Denmark the perfect place to put pedal power into practice.

BOAT IT ON NYHAVN'S WATERY BYWAY

HOLGER LEUE » LPI

LIFE-CHANGING EXPERIENCES

There's an old Scandinavian saying: 'The Danes live to eat, the Norwegians eat to live and the Swedes eat to drink.' Given the buzz that surrounds the New Nordic scene, it's easy to see that the Danes take their food very seriously. The image of Danish cuisine consisting of potatoes, dark bread, herring and cream has been ingeniously rebooted by adventurous chefs reworking Danish staples and techniques to produce unique dishes based on seasonal ingredients such as wild berries, plus beer-based sauces and Scandinavian wildlife. And the best place to try it is Noma, which is on the Copenhagen island of Christianshavn and was named the world's best restaurant in 2010. Chef René Redzepi's menu of modern twists on Scandinavian delights will make your senses swoon, but nabbing a table here is no mean feat – there's a waiting list of a few months. That said, you can count the city's other Michelin stars on two hands, and chef Rasmus Kofoed, of Geranium restaurant, won the Bocuse d'Or (World Cooking Contest) in 2011, meaning that if accolade-infused eating's your thing, then Copenhagen's your buffet table. Should all that inventive molecular cuisine have you yearning for the simpler pleasures, then Denmark's ubiquitous *smørrebrød,* the open-faced sandwich made of rye bread and embellished with all manner of toppings, will sate your appetite, or you can slake your thirst at one of the 200 microbreweries scattered throughout the country.

FESTIVALS & EVENTS

✪ The long-running Denmark by Design exhibition continues through to May 2013 at the Dansk Design Centre, focusing on the development and impact of Danish design from 1945 to 2010.

MARTIN LLADO » LPI

DESIGN FROM THE GROUND UP » RAPE FIELDS, SJAELLAND

○ On 5 May, Jutland's Herning plays host to the start of the Giro d'Italia. Denmark will then host two more stages of the race before it moves to Italy.

○ This year marks the 50th anniversary of Denmark's greatest writer of the 20th century, Karen Blixen (aka Isak Dinesen – *Seven Gothic Tales, Out of Africa*). The word is that famous director Bille August's biopic about Blixen will premiere in 2012. Set the scene by visiting the excellent Karen Blixen Museum (the home in which she was born and died) in Rungstedlund.

○ Strøget, the 1.1km car-free street, celebrates 50 years of being a pedestrian's paradise of snacking, shopping, street performance and people-watching.

RECENT FAD

The gritty slow-burning TV series *Forbrydelsen* (The Killing) has made a star out of Sofie Gråbøl. Her depiction of Detective Inspector Sarah Lund as she pursues the killer of young Nanna Birk Larsen, and matches wits with enigmatic politician Troels Hartmann (played by Lars Mikkelsen), will have you glued to the screen.

RANDOM FACTS

○ Denmark has two national anthems: 'Der er et yndigt land' (There is a Lovely Land) and 'Kong Christian stod ved højen mast' (King Christian Stood by the Lofty Mast).

○ Almost a quarter of all Danes have the surname Jensen, Nielsen or Hansen.

○ Until it was shut down in April 2010, Crown Prince Frederik's private Facebook profile went by the name of Jens Peter Hansen.

EUROPE

NORTH
AMERICA

ASIA

◇ BHUTAN

AFRICA

'Beautiful Buddhist Bhutan has always coyly shielded its charms from the wider world, but new areas are finally opening for business.'

by Sarah Baxter

06 BHUTAN

✪ **POPULATION** 708,427

✪ **FOREIGN VISITORS PER YEAR** 28,500

✪ **CAPITAL** THIMPHU

✪ **LANGUAGES** DZONGKHA, SEVERAL LOCAL LANGUAGES, TIBETAN AND NEPALESE DIALECTS

✪ **MAJOR INDUSTRIES** AGRICULTURE, TIMBER, HYDROELECTRIC POWER

✪ **UNIT OF CURRENCY** BHUTANESE NGULTRUM (NU)

✪ **COST INDEX** BOTTLE OF RED PANDA BEER NU90 (US$2), DAILY TOURIST TARIFF US$200-250, BOWL OF EMA DATSE (CHILLIES WITH CHEESE) NU35 (US$0.80), SOUVENIR THANGKA (BUDDHIST PAINTING) NU500-40,000 (US$11-1800)

WES WALKER » LPI

WHY GO IN 2012? SEE NEWLY OPENED AREAS OF THIS FABLED LAND

Things are afoot in the high Himalaya, and we don't mean the mighty yeti. Beautiful Buddhist Bhutan has always coyly shielded its charms from the wider world, but new areas of this remarkable mountainous land are finally opening for business.

Of course, you've been able to visit for years, but most tours hit the same highlights: a part-awesome, part-terrifying flight into peak-protected Paro, a jaunt around western Bhutan's cultural sights, then perhaps a trek through pristine mountains (Bhutan's conservation credentials are exemplary). There's no independent travel here; itineraries are sanctioned by the Tourism Council and guides are compulsory.

But now, at last, it's possible to visit other parts of this famously reclusive country. In a bid to raise tourist numbers, areas once off limits are being opened up. Royal Manas National Park, prowled by some of the planet's last remaining tigers, has reopened. And the far east, where most locals have seen more yetis than tourists, is accessible and is getting better infrastructure. You can join local spider-hatted Brokpa in the Merak Sakten region for butter tea at new tourist shelters, or experience a homestay in Trashi Yangtse.

It's also hoped that new festivals – celebrating seasons, valleys and odd-looking animals – will spread the visitor numbers (and *ngultrum*) across a wider swath of Bhutan.

The bad news? All this loveliness could cost even more. Bhutan has never been a budget destination, charging a tariff of US$200 per day (though this covers most on-the-ground costs). This figure is set to rise to US$250 in 2012, although at the time of writing, it wasn't a done deal; such an escalation doesn't sit well with global recession. If it doesn't happen, go quickly – the increase won't be deferred forever.

LIFE-CHANGING EXPERIENCES

The hike up to Tiger's Nest – Paro Valley's perilously perched monastery – is almost obligatory. Follow with a *tsechu* (festival) to see Buddhism at its most flamboyant, and then a trek up in them thar mountains: maybe a cultural hike in Bumthang, an offbeat expedition in the east or the full-on Snowman Trek, four weeks of high passes and Himalayan close-ups.

FESTIVALS & EVENTS

✪ The Bhutanese love a good *tsechu*, and these traditional festivals don't come bigger than Paro's in April, a colourful riot of costumes, music and exuberant masked dance.
✪ New shindigs to attract outsiders were inaugurated in 2011: Tshajarithang's Takin Festival bigs-up Bhutan's national goaty/moosey/antelopey animal in June 2012, while Haa's Alpine Festival in July celebrates the 'Mythic Valley of the Guardian Spirit' with yak rides and fiery home-brewed ara.
✪ Archery is Bhutan's national obsession. Tournaments take place across the country year-round, but given as it is the only sport in which Bhutan fields Olympians, all local eyes will be on London 2012...

RECENT FAD

Democracy. The Bhutanese have only had it since 2008 – largely because the people were pretty happy with their monarchy as it was. But the king himself decided to shake up the political process, and 2012 sees the first National Council elections since. Will democracy do the job?

HOT TOPIC OF THE DAY

Bhutan has historically had just one airport (finding flat land for a runway is quite a challenge), but that's set to change as part of the push to open up the east. New airports are planned in Bumthang and Yonphula, though it isn't entirely clear if they'll open in 2012. To complicate matters further, a new private airline was licensed to operate domestic flights, with no indication that national carrier Drukair would operate in competition. Then the private carrier dropped out, so now it's all back up in the air.

MOST BIZARRE SIGHT

Prudes, beware. There's much 'obscenity' to be seen here: many homes have a giant phallus daubed on their walls, or wooden appendages dangling from their eaves. But this is no nation of sexaholics – these seemingly dirty decorations are believed to ward off evil, as they represent Bhutan's saucy saint, the Divine Madman, who quelled a demon with his 'magic thunderbolt'.

GAVIN GOUGH »LPI

NORTH
AMERICA

EUROPE

ASIA

AFRICA

○ CUBA

'…it could soon be hello to a new Americanised Cuba, and goodbye to the quirky, quintessentially loveable Cuba.'

by Luke Waterson

07 CUBA

○ **POPULATION** 11.25 MILLION

○ **FOREIGN VISITORS PER YEAR** 2.5 MILLION

○ **CAPITAL** HAVANA

○ **LANGUAGE** SPANISH

○ **MAJOR INDUSTRIES** TOURISM, TOBACCO, MEDICAL PRODUCTS & SERVICES, NICKEL

○ **UNIT OF CURRENCY** CUBAN CONVERTIBLE PESO (CUC$) FOR MOST TOURIST COMMODITIES; ALSO CUBAN PESOS

○ **COST INDEX** CRISTAL BEER CUC$2 (US$2), ROOM IN A CASA PARTICULAR CUC$25-35 (US$25-35), INTERNET ACCESS PER HOUR CUC$6 (US$6)

KARL BLACKWELL » LPI

WHY GO IN 2012? GOING, GOING, GONE...

For years people have been saying it, and for years (53 and counting) the Castro brothers have staved off the inevitable – that Cuba has to change. Its socialist credentials are gradually crumbling in the face of international capitalism, as evidenced by dramatic public sector cuts and the relaxation of restrictions on private enterprise. With President Obama's increasingly tolerant attitude, it could soon be hello to a new Americanised Cuba, and goodbye to the quirky, quintessentially loveable Cuba. This is good news for Cubans, but bad news for fans of peeling Plymouths, crumbling colonial charm, impromptu salsa sessions in half-collapsed yet elegant houses, all-day coffee-and-rum breaks, and horse-drawn carts in the fast lane of highways. In short, everything that makes Cuba such a magical mayhem of contradictions is now under threat.

Even a few years ago, a sadness lurked behind the nonstop party atmosphere that permeates everyday Cuban life – understandable for a people who receive a world-class education but have precious few places to utilise it, and where beggars can make more than doctors. Now, as limiting laws are repealed, the optimism is palpable, but Cuba's soul is still hanging in there. And Cuba is all about soul. The beaches will still be pristine 10 years from now, and the world's best mojitos will still flow. But the country mightn't be quite so, well, distinctive. Or fun. Go while the clock is still stopped at 1959, and don't become one of those who can't join the conversation that starts: 'Remember Cuba before capitalism?'

LIFE-CHANGING EXPERIENCES

First soak up decrepitly grand, architecturally astounding, musically scintillating Havana. Marvel at the myriad art deco delights and contrast them with the monumental socialist contributions to the cityscape. Spice up your evenings by checking out a show at the legendary Tropicana or Vedado's ever-cool jazz club La Zorra y El Cuervo. Take in some hiking or horse riding in gorgeous Valle de Viñales, then add colonial sightseeing in Trinidad. Indulge in some of the Caribbean's best diving on Isla de la Juventud and always, always take a dose of the colourfully multicultural eastern city of Santiago de Cuba. You have the recipe for one hell of a holiday.

FESTIVALS & EVENTS

✪ Santiago de Cuba's carnaval in July is Cuba's biggest: a manic medley of fantastical floats and rumba that taps into the eastern city's exciting ethnic roots, where West Indian and African influences intertwine and blossom into the country's best festivity. The climax is on the 26th, the anniversary of Fidel's raid on the Moncada barracks, which effectively set the Revolution bandwagon rolling.

✪ Havana and jazz go together like rum and a Cuban cigar: at the city's Festival Internacional de Jazz in November umpteen renowned acts gather for performances in the leading theatres.

✪ Remedios gets Christmas Eve off to a cacophonous start with one of the Caribbean's most eclectic street parties, Las Parrandas; part carnival and part firework extravaganza, with the town split into two teams intent on out-revelling each other.

STEPPIN' OUT, CUBA STYLE

PATRICK SYDER » LPI

RECENT FAD

The internet. Cuba is bidding *adios* to the once-infamous queues for a few pricey state-controlled access points. In 2010 a high-speed cable to Venezuela (theoretically) gave people broadband for the first time. While online resources are appearing, if you're lucky enough to be allowed internet in your own home (many Cubans have to surf clandestinely), you'll still be treated with the reverence usually reserved for Fidel. OK, almost...

WHAT'S HOT...

Fidel (still). Overheating Cadillacs (still). Buenavista Social Club (still). The possibility of change (still).

WHAT'S NOT...

Beards (unless you're Fidel). Public transport. Political chitchat.

MOST BIZARRE SIGHT

Nothing embodies irony in Cuba like the little-visited ghost town of San Miguel de los Baños, a sadly ruined spa town in the verdant foothills of Matanzas province. Ostentatious hotels and houses shot up here in the early 20th century when the curative powers of the waters hit the headlines – until a sugar mill polluted the place. The wackily OTT buildings now lie abandoned, with livestock grazing within.

'…despite its fabulous islandscapes and unique mélange of Gallic and Melanesian cultures, New Caledonia rarely makes it onto travel shortlists.'

NEW CALEDONIA ✪

by Jean-Bernard Carrillet

08 **NEW CALEDONIA**

✪ **POPULATION** 246,000

✪ **FOREIGN VISITORS PER YEAR** 99,000

✪ **CAPITAL** NOUMÉA

✪ **LANGUAGES** FRENCH (OFFICIAL), KANAK LANGUAGES

✪ **MAJOR INDUSTRY** NICKEL MINING AND PROCESSING

✪ **UNIT OF CURRENCY** PACIFIC FRANC (CFP)

✪ **COST INDEX** PINT OF NUMBER ONE 500CFP (US$6), HOMESTAY IN A TRIBU 2000CFP (US$24), SINGLE DIVE 6500CFP (US$77), AIR CALÉDONIE PASS (FOUR COUPONS) 32,300CFP (US$385), PLATE OF LOBSTER 3000CFP (US$36)

JEAN-BERNARD CARPILLET » LPI

WHY GO IN 2012? TWO DESTINATIONS IN ONE

How strange it feels. You're greeted with a *bonjour* when you step off the plane, then you breakfast on croissants and baguettes at a pavement café in Nouméa – yet you're in the heart of the South Pacific. At first glance, New Caledonia resembles nothing less than a chunk of France teleported directly into the tropics. With its flurry of trendy shops, bistros, *boulangeries* (bakeries), shiny cars and upmarket marinas, Nouméa could be easily mistaken for city in the French Riviera. But beyond the *très* French panache of the capital and the west coast of the main island, Grande Terre, the indigenous Melanesian culture quickly comes to the fore. The rebirth of Kanak traditions has been gaining momentum for the past 30 years, and today is at an all-time high. Head to the Loyalty Islands or Ile des Pins and you'll enter another world. Richly steeped in Kanak culture, Maré, Lifou, Ouvéa and Ile des Pins are places where people live in clan communities known as *tribus* and dwell in cute-as-can-be *cases* (Kanak thatched houses) by idyllic beaches. In these rural settlements, the ancient Kanak code for living, *la coutume,* is very much alive. For the enquiring visitor, it's a fascinating opportunity to experience New Caledonia from a different perspective. Amazingly, despite its fabulous islandscapes and unique mélange of Gallic and Melanesian cultures, New Caledonia rarely makes it onto people's travel shortlists – which makes it all the more tempting to peek into.

NEIL FARRIN »CORBIS

LIFE-CHANGING EXPERIENCES

Close your eyes and imagine... You're aboard a traditional wooden *pirogue* that sails serenely across an aquamarine bay. You're dropped off at the far end of the bay where a path leads through an old forest to a clear blue pool cut off from the sea by a high reef. You don your snorkelling gear and you swim amid myriad tropical fish. Afterwards you head to a beachfront restaurant to feast on lobster. Idealised brochure material? No, just another day on Ile des Pins.

FESTIVALS & EVENTS

✪ Want to attend an authentic Kanak festival? Make a beeline for Festival of the Yam, which marks the beginning of the harvest around mid-March.

✪ If you're after something light-hearted, the Giant Omelette Festival, which is held close to Easter in Dumbea, may appeal to you. A dozen chefs, a huge skillet, 7000 eggs and many hands are used to make a free-for-all 3.5m omelette.

✪ Rodeos are always the highlight of rural agricultural fairs, such as Foire de Bourail in mid-August. It also features a cattle show, horse racing and a beauty pageant.

HOT TOPIC

Will it be one flag (a new purpose-designed standard) or two flags (the French alongside the Kanaky) for New Caledonia? This symbolic issue is proving very divisive in the context of building a national identity.

RANDOM FACTS

✪ *Roussette* (fruit bat) and *escargots* (snails) are considered local delicacies. Still hungry? Try *ver de bancoul* (a fat wood grub).

✪ The ribbon moray, a rare species of moray, has a yellow feather on its nostril and can be seen in New Caledonia's lagoon.

✪ Russa deer, introduced in the 20th century, have now reproduced to such an extent that they are creating major damage to the environment.

✪ The two tiny volcanic islands of Matthew and Hunter (respectively sitting 450km and 525km east of the southern tip of Grande Terre) have been the centre of a territorial dispute between Vanuatu and New Caledonia (ie France) since 1929. What's at stake? The increase in territorial waters.

MOST BIZARRE SIGHT

The cagou. This endemic flightless bird has an unusual call that sounds like a dog barking, which is ironic given that dogs are its main predator. Like the kiwi in New Zealand, this bird is an unofficial symbol for New Caledonia – guess how the country's sports teams are referred to when competing overseas? The cagou can be approached at Parc Provincial de la Rivière Bleue.

NORTH AMERICA

EUROPE

ASIA

 TAIWAN

AFRICA

'oversized sea cliffs and densely forested mountains…
the museums are simply bursting with treasures…plus
a thriving folk culture…'

by Robert Kelly

09 TAIWAN

- ✪ **POPULATION** 23 MILLION

- ✪ **FOREIGN VISITORS PER YEAR** 5 MILLION

- ✪ **CAPITAL** TAIPEI

- ✪ **LANGUAGES** MANDARIN, TAIWANESE

- ✪ **MAJOR INDUSTRIES** ELECTRONICS, MACHINERY, PETROCHEMICALS

- ✪ **UNIT OF CURRENCY** NEW TAIWAN DOLLAR (NT$)

- ✪ **COST INDEX** B&B DOUBLE ROOM NT$2000 (US$69), SHORT TAXI RIDE NT$150 (US$5.20), BIKE RENTAL PER DAY NT$400 (US$13.85), AFTERNOON OF OOLONG TEA FOR TWO NT$900 (US$31)

TONY WHEELER »LPI

WHY GO IN 2012? BIKING HITS THE BIG TIME

Taiwan has always had a jaw-dropping landscape – oversized sea cliffs and densely forested mountains barely start to describe its majesty. And then there's the museums, which are simply bursting with treasures (including the best of imperial China, spirited across the strait after WWII), plus a thriving folk culture that includes some wild displays of Taoist and Buddhist worship. In terms of cuisine, Taiwan is a fusion and slow-food showcase, with influences from across the island and greater Asia, all whipped up using the freshest of locally sourced ingredients.

Strangely enough, it was only in 2002 – after the first change in ruling parties for 50 years – that anyone thought about building a tourism industry around this heritage, and the world quickly took notice. Tourism numbers have more than doubled in the past 10 years, and even during the Asian economic crisis they grew by 18% a year.

So why is 2012 the time to visit? Because Taiwan is best seen on two wheels and in recent years the authorities have embraced the biking market with surprising enthusiasm, vision and (most importantly) funding. This year sees the linking of thousands of kilometres of paths, including two round-the-island routes, and a host of other cycling-friendly infrastructure projects. More than 40 countries also now enjoy visa-free entry, and while you won't find English widely spoken outside the cities, gestures such as big smiles and little acts of helpfulness will demonstrate just how welcome you really are.

LIFE-CHANGING EXPERIENCES

To understand why Taiwan was once called Ilha Formosa (the Beautiful Isle), ride up marble-walled Taroko Gorge: a Chinese landscape painting come to life. Better yet continue on to Wuling Pass (3275m), an 86km journey from the sea through forests of dripping subtropical vegetation to a final rolling alpine meadowland of dwarf bamboo. Fuel up along the way on local aboriginal fare like barbecued mountain pig and sticky rice steamed in bamboo tubes.

FESTIVALS & EVENTS

✪ In Donggang, believers in Wang Yeh (a collection of plague gods) gather every three years for a Boat Burning Festival to, yep, torch a 14m-long handcrafted ship. The Taoist rituals accompanying the ceremonies (in Oct or Nov 2012) are sublime.

✪ Follow a statue of Taiwan's patron deity on a tour of central Taiwan. The nine-day, 350km Matsu Pilgrimage (in late March or early April) showcases the local faith at its most devout, firework-friendly and exhausting.

✪ With celebrations that include dazzling laser shows and mass releases of paper sky lanterns, the Lantern Festival (two weeks after the Chinese New Year) draws in the crowds. The main events in 2012 will be held in the historic town of Lukang.

RECENT FAD

Though covering just 0.025% of the world's landmass, Taiwan possesses an astounding 2.5% of the earth's species of plants and animals. Plenty of land has been set aside to protect this natural heritage, and in recent years ecotours focusing on the many hundreds of bird and butterfly species have proven popular with North American and European travellers.

HOT TOPIC OF THE DAY

For many in Taiwan, the 2012 presidential elections have at stake nothing less than whether their island can remain free and independent from China's growing commercial, political and military clout. Only the environment could be a hotter issue: can this Asian tiger finally make the leap from heavy industry to a greener economy?

RANDOM FACTS

✪ Taiwan boasts over 15,000 temples, which is about the same, per capita ratio, as convenience stores.

✪ The Penghu archipelago is the windiest place in the northern hemisphere in autumn and is widely considered Asia's top windsurfing destination.

✪ Formed by the collision of two major tectonic plates, Taiwan is cursed with earthquakes but blessed with one of the world's highest concentrations of hot springs.

✪ Every winter some 10–15 million purple butterflies winter in the warm valleys around Maolin in the south.

MOST BIZARRE SIGHT

Yenshui's annual Fireworks Festival (two weeks after Chinese New Year) is noted for something mum definitely wouldn't approve of. The fireworks – big booming 'beehives' of them – are shot directly at you. Think of the event as running with the bulls at Pamplona and being asked not to move.

ORIEN HARVEY » LPI

'...you'll discover a Switzerland with art, attitude and an insatiable appetite for adventure. Goody two-shoes just doesn't get a look in.'

by Kerry Christiani

10 SWITZERLAND

- ✪ **POPULATION** 7.6 MILLION
- ✪ **FOREIGN VISITORS PER YEAR** 8.6 MILLION
- ✪ **CAPITAL** BERN
- ✪ **LANGUAGES** GERMAN, FRENCH, ITALIAN, ROMANSH
- ✪ **MAJOR INDUSTRIES** MECHANICAL AND ELECTRICAL ENGINEERING
- ✪ **UNIT OF CURRENCY** SWISS FRANC (SFR)
- ✪ **COST INDEX** CUP OF COFFEE SFR3.50-5 (US$4-6), MIDRANGE DOUBLE HOTEL ROOM SFR150-300 (US$178-355), ONE-DAY SKI PASS SFR55-75 (US$65-89), SLOPESIDE FONDUE IN A COSY ALPINE CHALET SFR20-30 (US$24-36)

DAVID TOMLINSON » LFI

WHY GO IN 2012? EPIC JOURNEYS AND ECO ANGELS

Whether it's economic growth, political stability or sustainable snow, little-miss-perfect Switzerland always finishes at the top of the European class. With its model railways, chocolate-box towns and outrageously beautiful mountains, the country should be the envy of all. But, critics say, doesn't perfect actually mean dull? Isn't Switzerland all holey cheese, skis and lights out by 10pm? Well, not quite.

Brush aside the stereotypes for a minute and the land of Heidi can also be hip. Stand in the wave-shaped shadow of Renzo Piano's Zentrum Paul Klee in Bern, party in Züri-West's industrial-chic clubs and experience a heart-stopping moment while glacier bungee jumping in Interlaken, and you'll discover a Switzerland with art, attitude and an insatiable appetite for adventure. Goody two-shoes just doesn't get a look in.

This year Switzerland's gloriously accessible Alps will become even easier to reach, thanks to the launch of 19 new TGVs from Paris, and the construction of the groundbreaking Gotthard rail tunnel getting underway. At higher altitudes, resorts are increasingly taking the green, car-free run; slow travel is feted on 60,000km of footpaths and the Jungfrau Railway, a romantically old-fashioned train line, will celebrate its centenary in 2012. *Der Weg ist das Ziel* ('The journey is more important than the destination') say the Swiss. And they're right, yet again.

LIFE-CHANGING EXPERIENCES

Switzerland is all about life that bit closer to nature. Send your spirits soaring as you schuss down Zermatt's freshly groomed slopes, the first rays spotlighting the perfect pyramid of the Matterhorn. Be awed by the icy grandeur of the 23km Aletsch Glacier and the thundering Rhine Falls, Europe's largest cataract. Or play among 3000m peaks in the solitary wilderness of the Swiss National Park, with a crisp blue sky overhead and only the marmots for company.

FESTIVALS & EVENTS

✪ Basel's Fasnacht is Switzerland's carnival must-see, with its torchlit processions, spectacular costumed parades, fifers and drummers. It kicks off at 4am on Monday 27 February.

✪ Half a million revellers get their groove on at Zürich's Street Parade (11 August), with love mobiles and DJs pumping out techno and house.

✪ On Monday 26 November, Bern's Zibelemärit (Onion Market) ushers in winter with 50 tonnes of tasty onions, confetti throwing and squeaky hammer head-bashing fun.

✪ Watch out as Santa wannabes in full costume battle it out in disciplines like chimney climbing and gingerbread decorating at the ClauWau championships in the Alpine village of Samnaun in November.

RECENT FAD

The latest back-to-nature trend is cow trekking, the brainchild of an organic farmer at Bolderhof in Hemishofen. Trekkers can saddle a Tyrolese Grey for a jaunt through bucolic countryside to the banks of the Rhine. Only in Switzerland...

ROOFS ARE FOR SKIING OFF, RIGHT?

CHRISTIAN ASLUND » LPI

HOT TOPIC OF THE DAY

Locals are still umming and aahing over EU membership and how it would affect the country's coffers and neutrality. Renewable energy is the burning issue in a growing number of alpine resorts as the impact of global warming kicks in.

RANDOM FACTS

✪ In 1943 Swiss chemist Albert Hoffman synthesised LSD while seeking a migraine cure. Despite the odd trip, he lived to the ripe old age of 102.

✪ There's no sea for miles, but Switzerland has 1500 crystal-clear lakes where you can take the plunge.

✪ Famed for their 'armed neutrality', the Swiss hate war but ironically love bunkers. Underground, the country is one gigantic nuclear shelter.

✪ Hiking yes, nude hiking...*nein*! Appenzell residents recently voted against allowing naturist ramblers, mostly from neighbouring Germany, to hike in their mountains.

✪ Hooray for Bollywood putting Switzerland's dreamy scenery on the map and doubling the number of Indian visitors in the past decade. From Geneva to Engelberg, the hills are alive with the sound of Hindi and the aroma of balti.

MOST BIZARRE SIGHT

Riederalp plateau in August: 500 residents, 17,000 cowpats and one hell of a Chüfladefäscht (Cow Pat Festival). This Valais village knows how to shovel shit with a smile. Bring your boots, garden spade or golf club for a day of dung-pulverising contests.

LONELY PLANET'S
TOP 10 REGIONS

© COASTAL WALES

EUROPE

NORTH AMERICA

ASIA

AFRICA

SOUTH

AUSTRALIA

'…walk the entire length of a country's coastline… trace its every nook, cranny, cliff-face, indent and estuary…'

by Sarah Baxter

01 COASTAL WALES

- ☼ **POPULATION** 2.2 MILLION

- ☼ **MAIN TOWNS** SWANSEA, ABERYSTWYTH, LLANDUDNO

- ☼ **LANGUAGES** WELSH, ENGLISH

- ☼ **MAJOR INDUSTRIES** TOURISM, AGRICULTURE, FISHING

- ☼ **UNIT OF CURRENCY** BRITISH POUND (£)

- ☼ **COST INDEX** B&B PER PERSON PER NIGHT £30-50 (US$50-83), PINT OF REAL ALE £2.90 (US$4.85), CASTLE ENTRY £3-6 (US$5-10), SURFBOARD HIRE PER DAY £10 (US$16.70), LAVER BREAD (SEAWEED MIXED WITH OATMEAL) £3 (US$5), POT OF COCKLES £3 (US$5)

HJW JONES » LPI

WHY GO IN 2012? ACCESS IT ALL

What a wonderful thing: to walk the entire length of a country's coastline, to trace its every nook, cranny, cliff-face, indent and estuary. How better to truly appreciate the shape – and soul – of a nation?

Well, in 2012 Wales will become the only country in the world where you can do just that. Due for completion in May, the All Wales Coast Path (AWCP) will squiggle continuously from Chepstow in the south to near Queensferry in the north – via dramatic serrations, candy bays and domineering castles – making 1377km of shore accessible.

Much of it is already in place, including the spectacular Pembrokeshire coast (a national trail since 1970); a new section from Llanmadoc to Port Eynon, passing Rhossili (one of the UK's best beaches); and the Isle of Anglesey Coast Path, waving to royals-in-residence Prince Wills and Kate on the way.

And as for the missing bits, the AWCP will soon fill in the gaps – announcing to locals and interlopers alike that this varied, increasingly vibrant seaboard is uninterruptedly open for business.

LIFE-CHANGING EXPERIENCES

The whole coast may soon be open, but Pembrokeshire's craggy edges remain a show-stealing starting point, with Barrafundle Bay and St David's (the UK's smallest city) particular highlights. You can also take in a glut of coast-protecting castles, such as Harlech, Caernarfon and Beaumaris, then learn to surf on the Gower Peninsula's perfect waves and amble around Anglesey. Wildlife buffs can seek out seabirds on the isle of Skomer and watch dolphins play off Cardigan Bay.

FESTIVALS & EVENTS

☼ Come 1 March, pin on your daffodil for St David's Day, when Wales' patron saint is toasted nationwide: Colwyn Bay hosts a parade and Swansea a weeklong festival. Alternatively, visit the main man's remains in St David's itself.

☼ Swansea's Maritime & Sea Shanty Festival (mid-July) is a salty affair – celebrate the sea port, dance a jig and watch the ships go sailing by.

☼ Wales' annual Eisteddfod – celebrating all things Cymru, from science and technology to music and dance – will be held a stone's throw from the sea in Llandow on 4–11 August.

☼ Soak up Olympic action in Wales: some of the London 2012 football matches will be held at Cardiff's Millennium Stadium.

RECENT FAD

Speaking Welsh. Unlike most minority languages, Cymraeg (Welsh) is on the up – more widely spoken now than in the 19th century. National TV and radio stations broadcast in Welsh, road signs are written in Welsh and English, and there are Welsh-medium schools, books and newspapers. Try Nant Gwrtheyrn centre, on the Lleyn Peninsula, for courses.

MOST BIZARRE SIGHT

Portmeirion. What's a town like this (part Italian riviera, part wedding cake, part surreal spy-thriller setting) doing on the Snowdonia coast? The fancy of architect Sir Clough William-Ellis, begun in 1926 and owned by a charitable trust, it delights and befuddles.

HUW JONES » LPI

LOCAL LINGO

At first glance Welsh words can seen bewilderingly strange, and unhelpfully short on vowels (though note that w and y are also vowels in Welsh), while poor old j, k, v, x and z don't exist at all. But it isn't so hard when you know a few rules – here's a quick primer:

Cymru Wales

shwmae hello

dioloh thanks

Iechyd da i chwi yn awr ac yn oesoedd Good health to you now and forever

tafarn pub

cwtch cuddle (once voted Wales's favourite word)

araf slow

Llanfairpwllgwyngyllgogerychwyrndrobwllllantysiliogogogoch OK, it's a place name, not a regular word. But it's brilliant.

REGIONAL FLAVOURS

Welsh food is having a moment. This land of plenty (all that rain has to be handy) nurtures succulent lamb, tasty beef and top-notch cheese and dairy. Traditionally it was served up with little ceremony (*cawl,* a meat and vegie broth, is typical). However, the gastro-bug has been caught, and innovative chefs are using Wales' bounty to better effect. Along the coast, look out for herring, mackerel, salmon and cockles. Brain's beer (brewed in Cardiff) is the tipple of choice, though Pembrokeshire's vineyards are starting to make a mark.

○ LA RUTA MAYA

'"Maya Mania" makes 2012 the ultimate year to check out the most mysterious ruins on earth.'

by Dan Savery Raz

02 LA RUTA MAYA, CENTRAL AMERICA

○ **POPULATION** YUCATÁN & CHIAPAS 8 MILLION, GUATEMALA 15 MILLION, HONDURAS 7.8 MILLION, BELIZE 307,899

○ **MAIN TOWNS** CANCÚN, GUATEMALA CITY

○ **LANGUAGE** CENTRAL AMERICAN SPANISH, ENGLISH

○ **MAJOR INDUSTRIES** TOURISM, COFFEE, SUGAR, BANANAS

○ **UNIT OF CURRENCY** MEXICAN PESOS (M$), GUATEMALAN QUETZALS (Q), HONDURAN LEMPIRAS (L), BELIZE DOLLARS (BZ$)

○ **COST INDEX** BOTTLE OF BEER US$0.70-3, THREE-HOUR BUS RIDE US$3.50-10, DOUBLE HOTEL ROOM US$8-35, WEEK OF SPANISH CLASSES WITH HOMESTAY US$100-200

TONY WHEELER » LPI

WHY GO IN 2012? APOCALYPSE NOW OR STAR TREK?

Where did the original Maya come from? Why did they disappear? No one really knows. But we do know that in medicine, mathematics and astronomy, the ancient Maya of Central America were galaxies ahead of the Old World. They developed a sophisticated water irrigation system, aligned their temples to form patterns with the stars and created a complex 13-month lunar calendar. This calendar is at the centre of 2012's end-of-the-world prophecies.

Archaeologists have long known that 21 December 2012 marks the end of the Mayan calendar's 'Long Count' (or 13th *baktun*) and the date is largely ignored by the modern Maya tribe. But 24/7 news, Hollywood movies and apocalyptic blogs have spawned some serious doomsday hype, though others say the date heralds a positive new era of human consciousness.

Whatever your view, all this 'Maya Mania' makes 2012 the ultimate year to check out the most mysterious ruins on earth. More of a universe than a region, La Ruta Maya (the Mayan Route) spans the Yucatán Peninsula and Chiapas in Mexico, plus Belize,

Guatemala and Honduras. The must-see Mayan cities include Tikal, Copán, Palenque and Chichén Itzá. But the lesser-known Cobá, Uxmal, Edzna and Yaxchilán are just as enchanting. So whether it's the end of the world as we know it or just another year, La Ruta Maya is always cosmic.

LIFE-CHANGING EXPERIENCES

The Mayan Route is not just about climbing pyramids in the jungle. It's also about scuba diving on a coral reef off the Caribbean island of Cozumel, brushing up your Spanish in the colonial city of Antigua, exploring the Mayan markets of San Cristóbal de las Casas, spotting howler monkeys in Jeannette Kawas National Park and swimming in the waterfalls of Agua Azul. For peace, top-up on tranquillity at Lake Atitlán, with its three dormant volcanoes, hang-out in a hammock in Tulum or soak up reggae vibes in the car-free island of Caye Caulker.

FESTIVALS & EVENTS

✪ The costumes are as colourful as the old colonial houses at Campeche's Carnaval in late February and early March.

✪ A gruelling five-day canoe race from the foothills of the Maya Mountains to Belize City, La Ruta Maya River Challenge in March is open to all.

✪ Chichén Itzá is the only place to be on the Vernal Equinox (20 March) and Autumnal Equinox (22 September), as sun and shadow create a serpent slithering down the El Castillo pyramid.

✪ Bonfires and fireworks light the night sky for Quema del Diablo (Burning of the Devil) in Guatemala on 7 December, representing the ridding of past evils.

WHAT'S HOT...

Holistic healing in Yucatán. Eco-resorts in Belize. Meditation retreats around Lake Atitlán.

WHAT'S NOT...

Bumpy 'chicken bus' rides in Guatemala. Hurricanes and eating Big Macs in Cancún.

RANDOM FACTS

✪ An estimated seven million indigenous Maya people live in Central America today, speaking over 21 different dialects.

✪ The temple rooftops of Tikal made a cameo appearance as the rebel base in the 1977 film *Star Wars*.

✪ *Popol Vuh* (the Mayan Bible) is one of the most significant Pre-Columbian American books and the name of an experimental 1970s German rock band.

✪ Belize (formerly British Honduras) is the only country in Central America where English is the official language.

UROS RAVBAR › LPI

MOST BIZARRE SIGHT

In the Guatemalan highlands, grown men tackle the Palo Volador (the Flying Pole), climbing to the top of tall pine poles erected in the town plaza and swooping around midair at the end of ropes. This dizzy dance takes place during the Fiesta of Santo Tomas (21 December) and comes from the Mayan tradition of *yaxche* – a mystical tree that unites the underworld, earth and heavens.

REGIONAL FLAVOURS

You can thank the Mayans for chocolate. The ancient inhabitants of Mesoamerica were the first people to cultivate cacao beans for a drink called *xocolatl*, which they mixed with chilli peppers. Today, Guatemalans still have a sweet tooth and the *flan de naranja* (orange flan) can be a dessert or served with eggs and tortilla at breakfast.

'…vast shattered lava deserts, camel herders…
hidden oases, fog-shrouded mountains…giant-tusked
elephants, barren islands dinosaur-like reptiles…'

AFRICA

○ NORTHERN KENYA

SOUTH
AMERICA

AUSTRALIA

by Stuart Butler

03 NORTHERN KENYA

○ **POPULATION** APPROX 2 MILLION

○ **MAIN TOWNS** ISIOLO, MARSABIT, LODWAR

○ **LANGUAGES** SWAHILI, ENGLISH

○ **MAJOR INDUSTRY** CATTLE

○ **UNIT OF CURRENCY** KENYAN SHILLING (KSH)

○ **COST INDEX** BUDGET DOUBLE HOTEL ROOM KSH600 (US$7), MEAL IN BUDGET
RESTAURANT KSH150 (US$1.70), ISIOLO–MOYALE BUS RIDE KSH1500 (US$17),
ENTRANCE TO SAMBURU NATIONAL RESERVE US$40, NIGHT IN LUXURY LODGE IN
SAMBURU NATIONAL RESERVE KSH16,600 (US$185)

DOUGLAS STEAKLEY » LPI

WHY GO IN 2012? THE ROAD TO NOWHERE?

For most visitors to Kenya the northern half of the country may as well not even exist, yet few other regions of Africa offer such extraordinary variety. This is a land of vast shattered lava deserts, camel herders walking their animals to hidden oases, fog-shrouded mountains populated by giant-tusked elephants, barren islands crawling with dinosaur-like reptiles, acacia woodlands teeming with wildlife and the jade waters of stunning Lake Turkana.

It is also an area of unforgettable adventure. Anyone venturing here should be prepared to challenge themselves against appalling roads, brain-melting heat, primitive food and accommodation, and vast distances to be travelled.

So why is 2012 the year to go? Those appalling roads that kept the northern area isolated from the heart of the country, and which lent such a sense of adventure to any travels, will soon be a thing of the past. A massive road construction project is underway throughout many parts of Northern Kenya. So if you wish to experience one of Africa's greatest adventures in all its dusty and pot-holed glory, 2012 might be your last chance.

LIFE-CHANGING EXPERIENCE

Any journey that involves blasting over a desert known as the plains of darkness en route to Lake Turkana cannot fail to be anything but life-changing. But though the scenery is spectacular, the wildlife abundant, the local tribal people fascinating and the adventure quota sky-high, it's not actually these things that make a safari to Lake Turkana so

CHRISTER FREDRIKSSON »LPI

extraordinary. Instead, thanks to the discovery of some of the oldest hominoid bones here, the Lake Turkana region can claim to be one of the birthplaces of the human race – a life-changing occurrence indeed.

FESTIVALS & EVENTS

✪ Held within the bounds of the Lewa Wildlife Conservancy each June, the Safaricom Marathon is a marathon with a difference. While most marathon runners are encouraged in their endeavours by cheering spectators, participants in this marathon are encouraged by the fact that if they're coming last they have a good chance of being eaten by a large toothy creature.

✪ If running away from animals isn't for you, get the animals to do the running for you at the Maralal International Camel Derby. Taking place over 10 days in early August, the slobbering steeds are available for rent so anyone can join in.

RECENT FAD

What do you do if your back garden covers a couple of hundred square kilometres? Well, in northern Kenya, where conservation is all the rage, you turn that spare patch of land into a private conservation area and open it up to discerning visitors seeking a very exclusive kind of safari. Some owned by the local communities and others by private concerns, these conservation areas are growing in number – many experts think that the future of conservation in Africa lies in such ventures.

HOT TOPIC OF THE DAY

North Kenya may look desolate, featureless and, in some eyes, worthless, but all that will change when the huge wind farm planned for Lake Turkana is completed in 2014. The 353 turbines will provide Kenya with 30% of its current total installed power and turn Turkana into the home of the biggest wind power project in Africa.

MOST BIZARRE SIGHT

Venture to the Central Island National Park, a volcanic island in the middle of Lake Turkana, and enter a real-life Jurassic Park where giant reptiles rule supreme. In this case it's crocodiles – lots and lots of them (some estimates say that 12,000 of them call Central Island home) and they're among the largest crocodiles in the world. You probably don't need to pack your swimming gear.

DEFINING DIFFERENCE

Northern Kenya is so utterly different from the rest of the country that even the animals look different. Ostriches that have pink legs in the rest of Kenya sport fetching blue ones here, giraffes alter their spots and yes, the zebra up in these parts really can change their stripes...

'…there's been no shortage of contenders for the title of "Lost Shangri-La", but now there's a new kid on the block: Arunachal Pradesh.'

by Stuart Butler

04 ARUNACHAL PRADESH, INDIA

✪ **POPULATION** 1.1 MILLION

✪ **MAIN TOWN** ITANAGAR

✪ **MAIN LANGUAGES** HINDI, ASSAMESE

✪ **MAJOR INDUSTRY** FORESTRY

✪ **UNIT OF CURRENCY** INDIAN RUPEE (RS)

✪ **COST INDEX** MIDRANGE DOUBLE HOTEL ROOM RS1300 (US$28), MEAL IN MIDRANGE RESTAURANT RS90 (US$2), SIX-HOUR BUS RIDE RS160 (US$3.50), TRAVEL PERMIT (FOR TWO PEOPLE) RS10,000 (US$220), JEEP RENTAL PER DAY RS3700 (US$80)

WHY GO IN 2012? THE LAST OF THE GREAT SHANGRI-LAS...

'Shangri-La is a mystical, harmonious valley', or so goes the description in James Hilton's 1933 novel, *Lost Horizon.* Hilton went on to describe a Garden of Eden on Earth: a land of milk and honey in a hidden Himalayan valley, where nobody grew old or ugly. Over the years there's been no shortage of contenders for the title of 'Lost Shangri-La', but now there's a new kid on the block: Arunachal Pradesh. Sitting exactly where India collides with Bhutan, Tibet and Burma, it's an ethnic, biological and geographical explosion of peoples, cultures, climates and landscapes – and is one of Asia's last great unknowns.

RICHARD I'ANSON » LPI

GETTING DOWN, MONK STYLE – NOVICES AT MORNING PRAYERS, TAWANG MONASTERY

A combination of rugged terrain, limited infrastructure and headache-inducing travel restrictions has meant that Arunachal Pradesh has been off the radar of all but the most determined (and cashed-up) travellers, but big changes are afoot. The good news is that travel restrictions have just been eased. Gone are the days of 10-day travel permits, minimum group sizes and weeks of waiting for permits to be issued; today even individual travellers can obtain one-month permits in a matter of days. With an expanding transport system, India's wildest state is ripe for the picking in 2012.

And what will today's traveller find there? The answer is thunderous Himalayan peaks so little-known that few have even been named, let alone climbed, plus jungles teeming with life forms that scientists are yet to catalogue (Arunachal Pradesh has the richest biodiversity in India), delicately tattooed and pierced tribal peoples living in longhouses in the forests, magnificent Buddhist temples and a severe dose of near limitless adventure.

LIFE-CHANGING EXPERIENCES

Long known as a 'forbidden valley', and home to the Buddhist Memba peoples, the fabulous Mechuka valley boasts an ancient Buddhist monastery and superlative mountain scenery. Travelling the newly opened road that links Mechuka to the rest of the state is quite simply one of the most exciting adventures in India.

FESTIVALS & EVENTS

The Torgya and Losar festivals (held in January and February, respectively) feature masked Tibetan Buddhist dances in one of the world's biggest Buddhist monasteries in Tawang.

RECENT FAD

As the Siang River emerges from the high Tibetan plateau and burrows through the Himalaya via a series of almighty gorges, it creates terrifying maelstrom of white water rapids that have recently been setting kayakers' hearts racing. The few who have so far taken to these waters report a 180km river descent littered with grade 4–5 rapids.

HOT TOPIC OF THE DAY

Arunachal Pradesh is an undeveloped region with little in the way of electricity, so the state government's announcement that will begin building a number of enormous hydroelectric projects is sure to brighten light bulbs throughout the state. On the flip side, pristine mountain valleys will be destroyed and environmentalists (as well as the government of the neighbouring state of Assam) are worried about the lack of proper environmental impact assessments.

LINDSAY HEBBERD »CORBIS

MOST BIZARRE SIGHT

Arunachal Pradesh is rumoured to be the home of the legendary Buddhist land of Pemako. A secret earthly paradise, Pemako can only be reached by passing behind an enormous hidden waterfall. And guess what? In the 1950s it was discovered that a huge hidden waterfall did indeed exist in Arunachal Pradesh and, what's more, beyond that was a rich and fertile valley populated by an isolated community of Buddhists.

DEFINING DIFFERENCE

This region is so different from most of India that it feels like a different country altogether, but nowhere is this more obvious than in the people. There are mountain Buddhists with a classically Tibetan appearance in the north, former headhunting Naga warriors in the east and in the centre are Apatani women who are reportedly so beautiful they disfigure themselves with facial tattoos and oversized nose and ear plugs.

REGIONAL FLAVOURS

Think India is all curries and chapattis? Think again. Culinary highlights of Arunachal Pradesh include barbecued rat and yak's milk tea, antelope captured in the forests and a delicious line in grubs, spiders and hornets.

EUROPE
○ HVAR

NORTH
AMERICA

ASIA

AFRICA

'...après-beach parties as the sun dips below the Adriatic horizon, full-moon shindigs and designer cocktails sipped seaside to fresh DJ-spun tunes.'

by Anja Mutic

05 HVAR, CROATIA

○ **POPULATION** 11,103

○ **MAIN TOWN** HVAR TOWN

○ **LANGUAGES** CROATIAN

○ **MAJOR INDUSTRIES** TOURISM, TRADE, AGRICULTURE, FISHING

○ **UNIT OF CURRENCY** CROATIAN KUNA (HRK)

○ **COST INDEX** SEASIDE COCKTAIL FROM 60KN (US$12), NIGHT IN PRIVATE ACCOMMODATION FROM 100KN (US$20), TAXI BOAT TO PAKLENI OTOCI 25KN (US$5), BOTTLE OF LAVENDER OIL FROM 20KN (US$4)

JEAN-PIERRE LESCOURRET » LPI

WHY GO IN 2012? IT'S CROATIA'S COOLEST ISLE

Come high summer, there's no cooler place in Croatia to get your groove on than Hvar Town on its namesake island. Fabulous suntanned bodies flock to this drop-dead-gorgeous spot for round-the-clock fun. Think après-beach parties as the sun dips below the Adriatic horizon, full-moon shindigs and designer cocktails sipped seaside to fresh

JONATHAN BLAIR » CORBIS

DJ-spun tunes. Croatia's party island really is as hot as the marble of the old town when the noon sun beats down. But you better rush to soak up all this glamour before Hvar becomes off-limits to mere mortals.

Best of all, on this Mediterranean flyspeck you can still get away from pulsating nightlife. For island bliss unmarred by glitz and bling, get into your birthday suit on the Pakleni Islands just offshore and – bikinis back on – explore the island's coastline and dreamy interior, with its endless fields of lavender, stretching sea vistas, towering peaks, scenic canyons and abandoned hamlets.

LIFE-CHANGING EXPERIENCES

There's more to Hvar than hobnobbing with celebs and pretty young things. On Croatia's sunniest isle (it gets 2724 sunny hours each year) you can ride scooters, swim, snorkel, dive, sail, sea kayak to isolated coves, hike up to the island's tallest peak of Sveti Nikola, mountain bike, rock climb and even tour off-road into the largely uncharted interior. If all the partying has pumped up your heart rate, try lofty pursuits of a different kind. Indulge the history buff in you by wandering the ancient Venetian grid of Hvar Town, where 13th-century walls surround ornamented Gothic palaces and winding marble streets. Check out the faded frescos and baroque loggias of Europe's oldest public theatre, this year celebrating its 400th anniversary. And don't skip the coastal towns of Stari Grad and Jelsa – more serene, cultured spots than their stylish big sister.

FESTIVALS & EVENTS

✪ Catch a spot of high culture in Hvar Town during Hvar Summer (mid-June to mid-October), when a repertory of drama, folklore performances and concerts alights various alfresco locations around town, including the cloister of the Franciscan monastery.

✪ Go all lilac during the annual Lavender Festival in the scenic Velo Grablje village the last weekend in June, a very local affair with exhibits, concerts and wine tastings.

✪ Indulge your wino tendencies on the last weekend of August at Jelsa Wine Festival, a two-day event showcasing homemade treats, the island's best wines and quirky entertainment such as a donkey race and tug-of-war.

✪ Pay respects to St Stephen, the town's patron saint, during Hvar Town Days on 2 October, with a post-Mass procession and concerts by *klapas* (Dalmatian a cappella groups).

RECENT FAD

Now that Hvar's gone all hoity-toity, you can spice up your stay with a bit of celebrity spotting. As A-listers sail in on their yachts every summer, it's become as common as the Hvar sunshine to spot Steven Spielberg, Gwyneth Paltrow, George Clooney or Kevin Spacey sipping a cocktail in one of the cafes that line the harbour. You won't find the paparazzi or screaming fans here, so snatch an autograph while you can.

WHAT'S HOT...

The après-beach parties at Hula-Hula – a boutique shack with a wooden deck on a rocky beach where all the young pretty things gather at sunset, fuelled by sun-downer cocktails and the sound of techno and house.

To soak up a more boho artsy vibe, head to – shhhhh! – Falko Bar, a pine forest beachside hideaway with a low-key vibe, homemade limoncello, swinging hammocks and occasional parties with live music and exhibits.

WHAT'S NOT...

Smack at the heart of Hvar Town, Carpe Diem, the mother of Croatia's coastal clubs, is now past its heyday and slightly frayed around the edges, so you better get your suntanned self over to the new Carpe Diem Beach on the island of Stipanska, now famed for its full-moon parties in summertime, peaking in August.

REGIONAL FLAVOURS

Think fresh seafood and fragrant Mediterranean herbs, all doused in top-quality olive oil and paired with tasty local wines. Don't skip *hvarska gregada,* the island's traditional fish stew served in many restaurants and best ordered in advance. Meat lovers should try the Dalmatian *pašticada* – beef stewed in wine and spices and served with gnocchi.

'...to experience Sicily's classic island charms before the whole place becomes a giant Ferrari and Alfa Romeo traffic jam, visit in 2012.'

by Gregor Clark

06 SICILY

✪ **POPULATION**: 5.1 MILLION

✪ **MAIN TOWN** PALERMO

✪ **LANGUAGES** ITALIAN (OFFICIAL), SICILIAN

✪ **MAJOR INDUSTRIES** AGRICULTURE, FISHING, TOURISM

✪ **NUMBER OF ACTIVE VOLCANOES** THREE

✪ **UNIT OF CURRENCY** EURO (€)

✪ **COST INDEX** ESPRESSO €0.90 (US$1.29), BOTTLE OF NERO D'AVOLA WINE €10 (US$14.30), CANNOLI €2 (US$2.85), CLIMBING TOUR OF STROMBOLI €28 (US$40)

STEFANO CELLAI » 4CORNERS IMAGES

WHY GO IN 2012? NEW ACCESS WILL CHANGE THE ISLAND FOREVER

The Straits of Messina have kept Sicily blissfully isolated for eons. Ever since Homer's *Odyssey* endowed these waters with the twin sea monsters Scylla and Charybdis, the Sicilians have counted on this treacherous passage to give them a little bit of breathing space from the rest of Italy. Leave it to Prime Minister Silvio Berlusconi to mess things up; in between sex scandals he's been working overtime to promote his pet construction project, a colossal bridge across the straits that will connect the Sicilian port of Messina with the tip of Italy's boot. Once completed, the 3.3km behemoth – with towers taller than the Empire State Building – will usher in a flood of new visitors.

If you want to experience Sicily's classic island charms before the whole place becomes a giant Ferrari and Alfa Romeo traffic jam, visit in 2012. For now, Sicily's end-of-the-world allure is still intact, and prices remain way lower than you'll find in Rome, Florence or Milan. Sunny weather, fruit-laden orchards and dozens of offshore islands give it an exotic southern Mediterranean vibe, while a treasure trove of temples, mosaics and ancient ruins ensure you won't feel starved for culture.

LIFE-CHANGING EXPERIENCES

Give yourself a couple of weeks to fully appreciate Sicily's eclectic appeal. Climb to the summit of Stromboli to watch volcanic fireworks lighting up the night sky; tour the jaw-dropping triumvirate of Greek ruins at Agrigento, Segesta and Selinunte; sunbathe on beaches lapped by turquoise waters along all three coasts (Ionian, Tyrrhenian and Mediterranean); visit the anti-Mafia museum in Corleone; and indulge your taste buds at every stop along the way.

FESTIVALS & EVENTS

✪ During Acireale's Carnevale (4–21 February), the streets in this baroque coastal resort come alive with gargantuan papier-mâché puppets, flowery allegorical floats, confetti and fireworks.

✪ In late May or early June, join Egadi Islanders as they circle their fishing boats and herd tuna into giant nets during La Mattanza (Ritual Tuna Slaughter).

✪ At the Taormina Film Festival (mid-June), modern filmmaker chic is juxtaposed against the ultra-retro backdrop of Taormina's ancient Greek amphitheatre.

HOT TOPIC OF THE DAY

Sicily's Mafia is fading fast. These days you're more likely find yourself dining on produce from government-confiscated Mafioso estates than getting mown down in the crossfire between rival gangs. Hundreds of businesses have begun resisting Mafia extortion as part of the *addiopizzo* ('goodbye bribes') campaign, and numerous Mafia kingpins have been arrested in recent years, most notably Bernardo 'the Tractor' Provenzano in 2006. On Christmas Eve 2010, even Santa Claus got into the act, slapping a pair of handcuffs on a very surprised mobster in Catania.

RANDOM FACTS

✪ Sicily is home to Europe's largest active volcano, Mt Etna (3329m), which dramatically blew its top yet again in January 2011.

✪ Linguists recognise Sicilian as a separate language, rather than a dialect. Take that, mainlanders!

✪ Sicily's unsettling official symbol, a gorgon's head surrounded by three legs, is called the trinacria, and was inscribed on Syracusan coins as early as the 4th century BC.

MOST BIZARRE SIGHT

People lining up to have their pictures taken in front of the metre-long *minchia* – a massive stone phallus – at Bar Turrisi near Taormina.

ALESSANDRO SAFFO » 4CORNERS IMAGES

DEFINING DIFFERENCE

Thanks to Sicily's prime position at the heart of the Mediterranean, you'll find traces of a dizzying array of cultures: Arab, Norman, Spanish, Greek, Byzantine and Phoenician, to name just a few. Even today Sicily remains a Mediterranean crossroads: in 2011 it became a major gateway for refugees fleeing the social upheavals in neighbouring Libya and Tunisia.

REGIONAL FLAVOURS

Sicily's cuisine bursts with flavours from the local landscape. Citrus, pistachios, almonds, capers, olives, eggplant, wild fennel, ricotta cheese and seafood find their way into everything from *caponata* to *arancini*. Other less-expected flavours hint at the island's North African ties, such as the chickpea fritters sold in Palermo's street markets or the fish couscous that rules the table in Trapani. If you have a sweet tooth, watch out: Sicilian desserts are wildly seductive, from *cassata* to *cannoli*, marzipan fruits to ice cream on a brioche; ditto for the region's sweet wines, including zibibbo, marsala and malvasia.

O MARITIME PROVINCES

'The tide is pulling especially strongly in 2012, when the Maritimes mark the 100th anniversary of the *Titanic* disaster.'

by Karla Zimmerman

07 MARITIME PROVINCES, CANADA

- ✪ **POPULATION** 1.8 MILLION
- ✪ **MAIN TOWN** HALIFAX
- ✪ **LANGUAGES** ENGLISH, FRENCH
- ✪ **MAJOR INDUSTRIES** FISHING, FORESTRY, OIL AND GAS, TOURISM
- ✪ **UNIT OF CURRENCY** CANADIAN DOLLAR (C$)
- ✪ **COST INDEX** GLASS OF BEER C$4.50 (US$4.70), DOUBLE B&B ROOM C$65-115 (US$68-120), LOBSTER SUPPER C$35 (US$36), WHALE-WATCHING CRUISE C$45-60 (US$47-63)

DAVID NUNUK » PHOTOLIBRARY

WHY GO IN 2012? BIG BITES & BOATS

Canada's Maritime Provinces – Nova Scotia, New Brunswick and Prince Edward Island (PEI) – have always exuded the quintessential briny vibe of clapboard fishing villages, clifftop lighthouses and townhall lobster suppers. But there's new action brewing. From distilleries popping up that turn PEI potatoes into silky vodka to organic farm wineries that crush Nova Scotia grapes into sweet vino, gastronomes are drinking up the rustic region. Stir in the wharfside oyster cafes, mushroom foraging tours and farmstead cheese-making classes, and you have a scene of plenty between sips, too.

The tide is pulling especially strongly in 2012, when the Maritimes mark the 100th anniversary of the *Titanic* disaster. The ill-fated ship struck an iceberg and sunk off Nova Scotia's coast on 15 April 1912, and many of those who died are buried in Halifax cemeteries. Commemorative events and museum exhibits with *Titanic* artifacts will be ongoing throughout the year.

LIFE-CHANGING EXPERIENCES

Celtic and Acadian communities dot the region, and their crazy-fiddlin' music blows the roof off local pubs, especially on Cape Breton Island. Tidal-bore rafting the extreme waves in Shubenacadie, Nova Scotia and fly-fishing the mythical rivers of Miramichi, New Brunswick are one-of-a-kind ways to work up a thirst. Better yet, whale watch in the Bay of Fundy, where the world's highest tides stir up serious fish food. Fin, humpback and endangered North Atlantic right whales (worldwide population: 400) swim in to feast, making a whale watch here extraordinary.

FESTIVALS & EVENTS

✪ Descendants of the Maritime's 17th-century French colonists tune their fiddles and unleash their joie de vivre for August's two-week Festival Acadien in Caraquet, New Brunswick.

✪ Join the oyster-shucking games or take the chowder challenge at PEI's International Shellfish Festival, in Charlottetown in mid-September.

✪ With foot-stompin' music amid riotous foliage, Celtic Colours rocks with nine days of big-name concerts, step-dancing classes and tin-whistle lessons at venues around Cape Breton Island in mid-October.

LET THE BRINY VIBE ROPE YOU IN AT PEGGY'S COVE, NOVA SCOTIA

RECENT FAD

Legal moonshine. Maritimers have long cooked up their own hooch using covert home stills, but PEI's Myriad View Distillery now produces the tonsil-singeing elixir lawfully for public consumption.

RANDOM FACTS

☺ PEI grows 1.3 billion kilograms of potatoes per year. That's 9300kg per resident, for those who are counting.

☺ Nova Scotia is the world's largest exporter of lobsters, Christmas trees and wild blueberries.

☺ New Brunswick holds several big records: the world's largest fiddlehead (an edible, asparagus-like fern), largest fake lobster and largest axe compete for stellar photo ops in Plaster Rock, Shediac and Nackiwac, respectively.

MOST BIZARRE SIGHT

The sight of Japanese women donning red pigtails then snapping photos by the dozen in front of a white-framed, PEI farmhouse might furrow your brow – until you learn that *Anne of Green Gables* is a Japanese pop-culture icon. The 1908 novel about a spunky redheaded orphan is set in the bucolic town of Cavendish, and more than 10,000 pilgrims jet over the Pacific each year to pay homage.

LOCAL LINGO

Listen for Scottish-tinged accents in rural Nova Scotia and PEI, and French inflections in New Brunswick (where French is the main language for about a third of the population). Lingo to know:

ceilidh (pronounced kay-lee) a raucous social gathering with Celtic music and dancing; sometimes called a 'kitchen party'

pets de soeur crunchy fried cinnamon rolls (whose name translates to 'nun's farts' in English)

REGIONAL FLAVOURS

Lobster is the Maritimes' main dish, boiled in the pot and served with a little butter. The best place to get cracking is in a PEI church basement or community hall supper club, where chunky potato salad, steamed blue mussels and a bulging slice of fruit pie round out the meal. Giant, butter-soft scallops from Digby, Nova Scotia show up on local menus, while Solomon Gundy and Lunenburg pudding are the province's acquired tastes. The former is pickled herring with onions; the latter pork and spices cooked in pig intestines (Scotch and water help to ease it down). In New Brunswick, hearty Acadian dishes hit the table, such as *poutine râpée:* baseball-sized grated potato dumplings filled with pork and drizzled with molasses.

'Where else can you ski in the morning and golf or water-ski in the afternoon?….Add excellent wineries and superb restaurants…'

by Craig McLachlan

08 QUEENSTOWN & SOUTHERN LAKES, NEW ZEALAND

- ✪ **POPULATION** 35,000
- ✪ **MAIN TOWN** QUEENSTOWN
- ✪ **LANGUAGE** ENGLISH
- ✪ **MAJOR INDUSTRIES** TOURISM, AGRICULTURE
- ✪ **UNIT OF CURRENCY** NEW ZEALAND DOLLAR (NZ$)
- ✪ **COST INDEX** BEER IN A PUB NZ$7 (US$5.60), MIDRANGE DOUBLE HOTEL ROOM NZ$150 (US$120), BUNGY-JUMP NZ$170 (US$136), LAKE CRUISE NZ$30 (US$24)

WHY GO IN 2012? THERE'S JUST SO MUCH GOING ON

There isn't a bad time to turn up in the world's top adventure playground. There's nonstop outdoor activities year-round in the resort towns of Queenstown, Wanaka and Te Anau, as well as the surrounding mountains, lakes and national parks.

It's not just the unbelievable alpine scenery. Where else can you ski in the morning and golf or water-ski in the afternoon? Head out hiking and drink water from mountain streams…then down more potent liquids in vibrant resort nightlife when the sun goes down. Raft down white-water rapids, tandem paraglide from craggy peaks or hike world-class trails such as the Milford, Routeburn and Hollyford tracks. View magnificent Milford Sound from the sky or on the water, jetboat up pristine rivers deep into snow-capped mountains, pull a rainbow trout out of a crystal-clear lake or pan for gold in secluded creeks. Add excellent wineries and superb restaurants, and what more is there to say?

LIFE-CHANGING EXPERIENCES

Acrophobics will have ample opportunities to cure their fear of heights as there's plenty going on in the skies – joy flights, hot-air ballooning, skydiving, paragliding, parasailing and hang-gliding. You can also abseil, zip-trek and even sky swing. And of course there's that Kiwi classic which was born in Queenstown: bungy-jumping.

Just stepping off the plane and staring up at the towering, rugged Remarkables mountain range is enough for some. If you take the dead-end road to Paradise from Glenorchy, at the head of Lake Wakatipu, you'll recognise the stupendous scenery that has featured in countless movies, magazines and television commercials all over the world.

ISABELLE VAYRON ⁄⁄ CORBIS

MAKE LIKE A COWBOY IN WANAKA

CHRISTIAN ASLUND » LPI

FESTIVALS & EVENTS

✪ Ride or run on the Motatapu Adventure, a top mountain-bike and off-road running event between Lake Wanaka and Arrowtown in early March.

✪ At Easter, the Warbirds over Wanaka Airshow will attract aviation enthusiasts from all over the world.

✪ Arrowtown's Autumn Festival in late April sees the town surrounded by scintillating colours and parades with dancing girls in the main street.

✪ Queenstown's pulsating Winter Festival, in early July, claims to be the southern hemisphere's biggest winter party. Gay Ski Week fills the town a few weeks later.

✪ In late October, Queenstown Jazzfest brings top jazz and blues artists to entertain in the mountain resort.

✪ Fitness fanatics descend on Te Anau in early December for the Kepler Challenge, a 60km mountain race over the Kepler Track that includes a 1200m ascent of Mt Luxmore.

WHAT'S HOT...

Disc golf in the Queenstown Gardens. The resort's popular (and free) frisbee golf course is attracting players of all ages and the discs are flying.

WHAT'S NOT...

Suits and ties. Forget your formal wear and relax in this mountain paradise.

HOT TOPIC OF THE DAY

Horror of horrors – Queenstown now has its first traffic lights, albeit to control traffic over a one-lane bridge.

RANDOM FACTS

✪ The region's lakes were formed by glacial action in the last ice age; after the giant glaciers retreated they left long, narrow, deep lakes. Queenstown's Lake Wakatipu is 84km long, 5km wide at its widest point and 420m at its deepest spot.

✪ Te Wahipounamu (Place of the Greenstone) is the southwest NZ World Heritage Area that encompasses four national parks and covers 2.6 million hectares.

✪ The kea, the world's only alpine parrot, is a cheeky, artful thief and vandal. It loves shiny key rings and to rip rubber off cars, especially windscreen wipers.

REGIONAL FLAVOURS

Deer farms concentrate around Te Anau. Try a succulent, tender venison dish. Wash it down with a decent tipple – some of the world's top pinot noirs are produced around Queenstown, Wanaka, Cromwell and Bannockburn. For the amber fluid, try microbrews from Wanaka Beerworks; Brewski, Tall Black and Cardrona Gold all get rave reviews. And Berriman's Cider, made from local apples, is a big hit on hot summer days.

'...the nexus of varied activities, exotic locales, excellent food and cultural diversity come together in a cocktail of very affordable fun.'

© BORNEO

by Shawn Low

09 BORNEO

○ **POPULATION** 18.8 MILLION

○ **MAIN TOWNS** KUCHING (SARAWAK), KOTA KINABALU (SABAH), SAMARINDA (EAST KALIMANTAN), BANJARMASIN (SOUTH KALIMANTAN)

○ **LANGUAGES** BAHASA MALAYSIA, BAHASA INDONESIA (BOTH OFFICIAL), INDIGENOUS LANGUAGES, ENGLISH, CHINESE DIALECTS

○ **MAJOR INDUSTRIES** TOURISM, TIMBER, OIL, PALM OIL

○ **UNIT OF CURRENCY** MALAYSIAN RINGGIT (RM), BRUNEI DOLLAR (B$), INDONESIA RUPIAH (RP)

○ **COST INDEX** TIGER BEER US$3, MIDRANGE DOUBLE ROOM FROM US$20, KEDAI KOPI MEAL US$2-3, ENTRY SEPILOK ORANG-UTAN REHAB CENTRE US$10

SABINE HENG » LPI

WHY GO IN 2012?
TROPICAL PARADISE ON THE CHEAP

Borneo is to Malaysia and Indonesia as Hawai'i is to the USA – a tropical island getaway. And the secret is nearly out: Borneo is one of the last remaining tropical paradises that won't break the bank. The East Malaysian states of Sabah and Sarawak, tiny but oil-rich Brunei and Indonesian Kalimantan are home to the world's oldest rainforests, the region's third-highest peak and some of the world's best diving. The indigenous Dayak peoples add a layer of intriguing cultural complexity and, of course, there is also that cutest of primates – the cheeky orang-utan.

Better still, your budget will go a long way here. A typical meal in a local coffee shop will only set you back US$2 and tourist numbers are only 10% that of mainland Malaysia or Indonesia.

Borneo is that rare place where the nexus of varied activities, exotic locales, excellent food and cultural diversity come together in a cocktail of very affordable fun.

LIFE-CHANGING EXPERIENCES

Ascending the region's highest peak, Sabah's Mount Kinabalu, to catch the sun breaking over lofty clouds seems a world away from watching sea turtles and reef sharks drift by while you dive Sipadan's vertical walls. The scenery changes again in Sarawak, where you can trek deep into 130-million-year old tropical rainforest to stay in an indigenous longhouse. Of course, if you're not into sweating, you could simply find your own white-sand beach getaway at coral-ringed Pulau Mantanani. And for a true step back in time, explore the dense jungles of Indonesia's Kalimantan – and find your Southeast Asian equivalent of Conrad's *Heart of Darkness*.

FESTIVALS & EVENTS

✪ Gawai Dawak is the annual harvest festival held in Sarawak (31 May to 2 June). Local tribes mark the end of rice season by donning colourful traditional dress and hosting war dances, cockfights and blowpipe events. Expect liberal dispensing of rice wine. To refuse is to be impolite. You've been warned.

✪ The Sarawak Cultural Centre is a living museum showcasing indigenous culture. For three days in July or August, it is also home to the Rainforest World Music Festival, a music and arts festival with an indigenous bent.

SABINE HENG » LPI

FISHING IS A FAMILY AFFAIR FOR BAJAU LAUT SEA GYPSIES, PULAU MABUL

⊙ Held in late September, the Erau Festival in Kalimantan sees thousands of Dayaks converging on Tenggarong in a whirlwind of tribal costumes and ritual dancing. It's one big intertribal party.

HOT TOPIC OF THE DAY

Deforestation. Tropical rainforest is being cut away in order to free up land for productive palm-oil trees. Slash-and-burn techniques practised by some farmers also contribute to environmental degradation. With such a variety of unique wildlife, Borneo has an illicit animal trade that was reported to be worth US$1.3 billion as of 2004. Thankfully, there are various animal protection and conservation groups in operation.

RANDOM FACTS

⊙ The first season of Survivor was shot on Pulau Tiga, Sabah
⊙ There is no record of any human entering the Maliau Basin until the 1980s.
⊙ Borneo is only one of two places in the world where the orang-utan is found. The other is Sumatra.
⊙ The lavish Empire Hotel & Country Club in Brunei cost US$1.1 billion to build. Ahh, there's no money like oil money.

MOST BIZARRE SIGHT

Orang-utans might be the most popular primates here, but the proboscis monkeys are stranger looking. Found only in the jungles of Borneo, the males have a long, almost-bulbous nose that stretches up to 18cm. Coupled with a huge, swollen belly, this monkey is a certainly a head turner. The rafflesia flower, a rare plant that emits a stench of rotting flesh when flowering, comes a close second.

LOCAL LINGO

Bahasa Malaysia and Indonesia are very similar. Since they are both phonetic languages that are written with the English alphabet, most visitors can take a stab at pronouncing words, although minute differences in pronunciation can have hilarious results:

jemput/jembut the former means to 'call for'; the latter 'pubic hair'
penjahit/penjahat tailor or criminal
wortel/wartel carrot or telephone service
panas/pedas hot (temperature) or hot (spice); could mean the difference between searing your tongue with chilli or not
kepala desa/kelapa desa village head or village coconut; be careful what you ask for
senang sekali/sayang sekali 'very happy' or 'sorry to hear that'; not to be confused when conveying condolences

'…this is a place where you can slow the pace right down, settle in and indulge in the finer things life has to offer.'

by Stuart Butler

10 POITOU-CHARENTES, FRANCE

- ✪ **POPULATION** 1.72 MILLION
- ✪ **MAIN TOWN** LA ROCHELLE
- ✪ **MAIN LANGUAGE** FRENCH
- ✪ **MAJOR INDUSTRIES** FARMING, MACHINERY PRODUCTION, CHEMICAL PRODUCTION, TOURISM
- ✪ **UNIT OF CURRENCY** EURO (€)
- ✪ **COST INDEX** MIDRANGE DOUBLE HOTEL ROOM €80-90 (US$113-127), MENU DU JOUR IN MIDRANGE RESTAURANT €12 (US$17), ESPRESSO €1 (US$1.43), KAYAK RENTAL IN MARAIS POITEVIN €12 (US$17), ENTRY TO LA ROCHELLE AQUARIUM €13 (US$18)

WHY GO IN 2012? TO ENJOY THE FINER THINGS IN LIFE

With quiet country roads wending through vine-striped hills and wild stretches of coastal sands interspersed with misty islands, the Atlantic coast is where the French get back to nature. Much more laid-back than the Med (but with almost as much sunshine) and ideally suited to family holidays, this is a place where you can slow the pace right down, settle in and indulge in the finer things life has to offer.

And there are numerous ways in which to do this. You could spend a morning quietly greeting curious ducks as you kayak down the glowing green canals, rivers and streams of the Marais Poitevin. You could cycle over the lazy landscapes of the dreamy Île de Ré or raise a glass in the pretty town of Cognac. Or soak up the salty air of the white city, La Rochelle, after exploring its fascinating museums and breathtaking aquarium.

Poitou-Charentes is far from undiscovered – French tourists have been flocking here for years – but aside from the city of La Rochelle (an increasingly popular weekend break destination thanks to arrival of budget airlines), the area is woefully under-visited by foreigners. So get there now before the weekend breakers realise what they're missing.

PUKU » CORBIS

OH WELL, SOMEONE'S GOT TO DO IT – AND THE COGNOSCENTI CLUSTER IN COGNAC

LIFE-CHANGING EXPERIENCES

A visit to La Rochelle's state-of-the-art aquarium uses interactive displays, films and all manner of weird and wonderful sea creatures to illustrate how humans are using and abusing the oceans of the world. Happily, it also suggests what we need to do in order to save all the critters that live within them.

FESTIVALS & EVENTS

✪ La Fête du Cognac is four days of adult- and child-friendly mayhem that fills the streets of Cognac in mid-July.

✪ The Festival International du Film screens silent classics as well as new nondubbed films during La Rochelle's 10-day film festival in early July.

✪ Francofolies is a cutting-edge, contemporary music and performing arts festival held over four days in La Rochelle in mid-July.

✪ OK, so Les Sables d'Olonne is in the neighbouring department of the Vendée, but the start of the Vendée Globe Round the World Race on 21 October is just a short drive from equally boat-crazy La Rochelle.

RECENT FAD

The Marais Poitevin has long been something of a forgotten backwater, but today increasing numbers of domestic French tourists are discovering this tranquil bird-filled wetland dubbed the Venise Verte (Green Venice) due to the duckweed that turns its

JEAN-LUC BOHIN » PHOTOLIBRARY

maze of waterways emerald green each spring and summer. If you want to discover the slow beat of rural France, there are few better places to do it.

MOST BIZARRE SIGHT

If a museum dedicated to dolls sounds a little like child's play, then think again – with dozens of walking, talking and almost living dolls, La Rochelle's Musée des Automates is actually one of the most surreal and interesting museums in France. Eat your heart out Barbie!

DEFINING DIFFERENCE

What makes Poitou-Charentes so different from the rest of France is that it encapsulates the best of France in one small, easily digestible region. Put simply, Poitou-Charentes combines all the best clichés of the French countryside – the sleepy rural villages, the endless fields of sunflowers and the delicious food and drink – and this alone makes it different from every other region in the country.

REGIONAL FLAVOURS

The food and drink of this region is legendary. Seafood is the star attraction around La Rochelle, with nearby Île de Ré renowned for its oysters. To combine taste-bud satisfaction with sightseeing, a visit to the distilleries and museums of the pretty cobbled town of Cognac, home of you know what, should be high on your list of places to visit.

094
LONDON

098
MUSCAT

102
BENGALURU

106
CÁDIZ

110
STOCKHOLM

LONELY PLANET'S
TOP 10 CITIES

114
GUIMARÃES

118
SANTIAGO

122
HONG KONG

126
ORLANDO

130
DARWIN

○ LONDON

EUROPE

NORTH AMERICA

ASIA

AFRICA

AUSTRALIA

'…it's going for the knock-out blow in 2012. The Olympics are riding into town…'

by Tom Hall

01 LONDON, ENGLAND

○ **POPULATION** 7.8 MILLION

○ **FOREIGN VISITORS PER YEAR** 14.6 MILLION

○ **LANGUAGE** ENGLISH

○ **UNIT OF CURRENCY** BRITISH POUND (£)

○ **COST INDEX** PINT OF REAL ALE £2.80 (US$4.55), BUDGET DOUBLE HOTEL ROOM £70-90 (US$115-148), SHORT TAXI RIDE £10 (US$16.30), CHEAPEST TICKET FOR OLYMPICS £20 (US$32.40)

JANE SWEENEY »LPI

WHY GO IN 2012? LONDON'S OLYMPIC YEAR

London is a pugnacious so-and-so, and after a little light sparring with the world's great cities in 2011 (did someone mention a royal wedding?), it's going for the knock-out blow in 2012. The Olympics are riding into town, with London becoming the first city to host the games three times, and a whole swath of the capital is being transformed in the process.

Forget the usual rule of an Olympic city: overpriced rooms that are booked out before a flurry of last-minute deals. London will be popular, but it has room for everyone, whether you get in quick with an early-bird hotel deal, stay a few miles out and travel in for the day, or blag a stay with a Londoner in a surprising suburb.

London's east will be thrust into the spotlight (and Shoreditch, Hoxton and Dalston are all worth exploring by night), but the rest of the capital will be rolling out the red carpet, too. Even if sport's not your bag, it's still worth visiting – queues at some of the world's best museums and galleries should be a little shorter as the Games divert everyone's attention.

LIFE-CHANGING EXPERIENCES

Seeing Tower Bridge lift its bascules to let a tall ship pass beneath is all stately grace, as opposed to your first rush-hour trip on the tube, getting up close and personal with strangers of every colour, creed and nationality, all shoving their noses into each other's armpits. Mind the gap! And of course roaring on your heroes in the Olympic Stadium, velodrome or swimming pool will get the adrenaline flowing – whoever you cheer for you, won't be alone in this most international of cities.

FESTIVALS & EVENTS

✪ Queen Elizabeth II celebrates 60 years on the throne with her Diamond Jubilee on 2–5 June. On Sunday 3 June she will lead a flotilla of 1000 ships, smaller boats and self-propelled craft along the Thames.

✪ The Games of the XXX Olympiad, or London 2012 to you and me, take place from 27 July to 12 August, with the XIV Paralympic Games running from 29 August to 9 September.

✪ The Mayor of London hosts the Thames Festival on 8 and 9 September. This is London's largest outdoor arts festival with music, dancing, street arts, river races and a carnival. It's an excellent excuse to get out on the river.

RECENT FAD

Londoners have been quick to embrace Boris Bikes. Informally named after the former mayor who launched the scheme, Boris Johnson, these three-geared, blue-and-grey bad boys have quickly become a familiar sight. The bikes' ubiquity in the central area mean that a ride in a black cab may become London's equivalent of a gondola ride – do it once, then use your own legs the rest of the time. Once you're registered, the first 30 minutes of any journey is free.

WHAT'S HOT...

Hipster cycling cafes. Have an espresso while your gears are recalibrated by a nattily dressed grease monkey.

WHAT'S NOT...

The statue of Michael Jackson at Fulham FC's Craven Cottage ground. It's a source of great hilarity for visiting fans.

HOT TOPIC OF THE DAY

The Shard London Bridge, the new tallest building in the UK, is slated to open in May. Opinion is divided over this and other skyscrapers popping up in the capital, not least because Renzo Piano's irregular triangle will inevitably change some iconic views.

STAIRING IS DE RIGUEUR AT CITY HALL

NEIL SETCHFIELD » LPI

MOST BIZARRE SIGHT

Around dawn on most days, British Army cavalry regiments quartered nearby exercise their horses on the Outer Circle road around Regent's Park, with the sweaty, noisy troop scaring the life out of early-morning joggers.

CLASSIC RESTAURANT EXPERIENCE

Is there anywhere more British than Rules? This Covent Garden institution dates back to 1798, which makes it not just London's oldest restaurant but also older than many countries. This is classic English dining (think steak and oyster pie) but offers a few quirky flashes, such as a cocktail named after Kate Middleton.

CLASSIC PLACE TO STAY

St Pancras Station is one of London's best-loved buildings, and those arriving on the *Eurostar* can now flop straight into the St Pancras Renaissance London. Occupying the space once used by the Midland Grand Hotel, this top-end refit has rapidly become one of the capital's most drooled-over destinations.

'…a luxury break with history and mystery laid on, but also a certain naive charm.'

by Luke Waterson

02 MUSCAT, OMAN

✪ **POPULATION** 1.1 MILLION

✪ **FOREIGN VISITORS PER YEAR** 1.5 MILLION

✪ **LANGUAGES** ARABIC (OFFICIAL), ENGLISH

✪ **BEST TAKE-HOME GIFTS:** PERSIAN RUGS, KHANJARS (CEREMONIAL DAGGERS), FRANKINCENSE, DATES, 19TH-CENTURY COINS REFLECTING MUSCAT'S POSITION ON THE OLD CARAVAN TRADING ROUTES

✪ **UNIT OF CURRENCY:** OMANI RIAL (OMR)

✪ **COST INDEX:** BUDGET DOUBLE HOTEL ROOM OMR27 (US$70), TOP-END DOUBLE HOTEL ROOM OMR105 (US$275), CROSS-TOWN TAXI RIDE OMR5 (US$13), MEAL IN A BUDGET RESTAURANT OMR5-7 (US$13-18)

CESARE GEROLIMETTO »CORBIS

WHY GO IN 2012? EXPLODING ONTO THE EXOTIC HOLIDAY SCENE...

While the Western world recovers from the economic crisis, Oman is firing on all fronts
to attract international visitors, expanding everything from its museums to its resorts.
Muscat is the focus for the revamp, with cultural events, luxury accommodation
and aquatic activities taking centre stage. In 2010 the 40th-anniversary celebrations
of Sultan Qaboos' ascension provided a focus for the country's traveller-enticing
potential, particularly through the Asian Beach Games and the Tour of Oman cycle
race, as well as the Muscat Festival, which has garnered a global following, thanks to
prestigious sideshows such as an inaugural fashion week (aiming to put Muscat at
the pinnacle of Arabian fashion) and the Extreme Sailing Series (the world's toughest
sailing odyssey). Now the talk has been talked and the cranes cleared off. Muscat in
2012 is settling into its new place on the world stage. Now it's about Qurum's trendy
designer outlets, Old Town souks and wacky water sports enlivening its coastline
alongside traditional dhows (and the odd Qaboos-owned luxury yacht).

So why head off to this most historically riveting of the great Gulf cities? Well, aside from fancy hotels like the Millennium Resort and a stonking new Royal Opera House sharing the skyline with the minarets and 16th-century forts, development is a new animal here. So new that it's making Dubai and Abu Dhabi seem old hat. Unlike its more blasé metropolitan cousins, Muscat has only been enjoying serious tourism a few years, so much of the city is unchartered waters as far as mainstream holiday promotion goes. For the moment it offers a luxury break with history and mystery laid on, but also a certain naive charm. Muscatis are still genuinely interested to see visitors, so much so first-timers might have the odd feeling of being welcomed *back*: like returning to the house of an old friend. In Muscat's case, it's a friend that's changed unrecognisably in just 40 years. 'Tomorrow will be a new dawn on Muscat,' the Sultan pledged upon attaining power in 1970. Today in Muscat, the sun has well and truly risen.

LIFE-CHANGING EXPERIENCES
Few cities blend the ultramodern and the traditional as effortlessly as Muscat, where both nestle under the all-pervading white sheen of the buildings spreadeagled along a sparkling mountain-backed coast. So whether you fancy spa pampering, gawping at the phenomenal Grand Mosque or climbing the umpteen ancient forts crowning precipitous headlands on the municipality's shoreline, Muscat can oblige. But the city doesn't understand roughing it: luxury is never far away. This even applies to the legendary sand dunes of Rub' al Khali (the Empty Quarter). You'll likely be reclining with a wickedly strong coffee in your swanky desert camp thinking: did Lawrence of Arabia really have it so tough?

FESTIVALS & EVENTS
✪ Muscat Festival in January/February is an extravaganza encompassing everything from cuisine and handicrafts demos to fashion parades, mainly set against the lush backdrop of Qurum National Park.
✪ Oman's National Day on 18 November doubles as a celebration of the birthday of both the Sultan and the country itself. With camel-racing and blow-up pictures of the Sultan everywhere, it's certainly a spectacle.

WHAT'S HOT...
The coffee (and sipping it on Muttrah sidewalk cafes looking cool). Big 4WDs. Designer shopping in Qurum.

STEPHANIE RABEMIAFARA » CORBIS

WHAT'S NOT...

Binge drinking. Speculating on the Sultan's sexuality. Refusing to haggle in souks.

MOST BIZARRE SIGHT

It might not appear remarkable to Western eyes, but Muscat's 'Old Road' is endearingly touted as a must-see sight. It's not even that old, yet it enjoys a reputation as some of the only paved kilometres of carriageway to have existed before the 1970 shake-up in Oman. Wow... But the views of city are superb from here. Proper wow.

CLASSIC RESTAURANT EXPERIENCE

Have your first meal out at the Mumtaz Mahal; you won't regret climbing the bluff behind Qurum National Park to this top-notch, top-nosh Indian eatery. Inside the slick, spacious glass-walled interior, chow down on a Chennai *murg masala* (chicken with coconut) and finish with the famed snake coffee, prepared flambé-style at your table.

○ BENGALURU
(BANGALORE)

'…tech-savvy Bengaluru offers the choicest cosmopolitan pleasures to make visitors feel at home.'

by Anirban Mahapatra

03 BENGALURU (BANGALORE), INDIA

○ **POPULATION** 5.8 MILLION

○ **FOREIGN VISITORS PER YEAR** 340,000

○ **LANGUAGES** ENGLISH, KANNADA, HINDI

○ **POPULAR CATCHPHRASE** MAADI (VERB; USED AS A SUFFIX MEANING 'TO DO')

○ **UNIT OF CURRENCY** INDIAN RUPEE (RS)

○ **COST INDEX** PINT OF BEER RS55 (US$1.25), MIDRANGE HOTEL DOUBLE ROOM RS2000 (US$45), SHORT AUTORICKSHAW RIDE RS70 (US$1.50), ADMISSION TO THEATRE OR PUB GIGS RS200 (US$4.50)

WHY GO IN 2012? THE CHILL DRILL

The undisputed Elvis of South Asian megacities, Bengaluru is in a class of its own when it comes to redefining flamboyance. Perpetually drunk on the good life, this South Indian metropolis packs in the best brews, the scrummiest cuisines, the trendiest shopping malls and the liveliest arts and music scene, not to mention the hippest population you could hang out with. Move over Delhi and Mumbai – Bengaluru's stolen your fizz. And this year, evenings in the 'capital of cool' are poised to get even more intoxicating.

MANJUNATH KIRAN » CORBIS

YOU WANT FIREWATER? WE GOT IT

Home to both the UB Group (India's numero-uno brewmasters) and an ever-increasing community of white-collar expats, tech-savvy Bengaluru offers the choicest cosmopolitan pleasures to make visitors feel at home. Want a heads-up on the newest hot spots? Well, there's Skyye Bar, a super-stylish lounge at dizzying heights, with bird's-eye views of the city below; and Touche Diner, the first of its kind in India offering gizmo-aided fine-dining. English Premier League fans can check out the Manchester United Restaurant Bar, complete with a stadium tunnel and dugouts. And if the maddening traffic has always been your concern, take heart: Bengaluru's new high-speed Metro network now ensures that your favourite watering hole is easier to reach than ever. There's only one thing you could say to that: 'Chill *maadi!*'

LIFE-CHANGING EXPERIENCES

Breathe pure oxygen on a leisurely stroll in the sylvan environs of Cubbon Park. Hone your photographic skills while being bowled over by the timeless sights and sounds of colourful Krishnaraja Market. Overcome sticker shock and shop away your last pennies at the uberswanky UB City shopping mall, or gawk in juvenile wonder at a motley squadron of aircraft at the HAL Aerospace Museum & Heritage Centre. Then grab a seat at the M Chinnaswamy Stadium and witness a high-octane Twenty20 cricket match, before calling it a day over fresh draught at a happy MG Road pub.

FESTIVALS & EVENTS

✪ The city's festive calendar kicks off in January with Bengaluru Habba, a two-week cultural gala featuring a barrage of music concerts, dance events, movie screenings, theatre performances, and art and craft fairs. And all of it is free!
✪ Tipplers can go on a rampage in March, when the three-day International Wine Festival celebrates the finest Indian nectars with much fun and frolics.
✪ In October, the annual Ranga Shankara Theatre Festival treats the city's theatre aficionados to the best of contemporary and classic Indian stage productions.

RECENT FAD

Jeffrey Archer billed RK Narayan as his favourite Indian English-language author on a recent fly-by. Needless to say, the back catalogue of the legendary Kannada novelist suddenly seems back in demand among the city's bookworms. So pair your cappuccino with a copy of *Swami and Friends*, and laze away the afternoons in style.

WHAT'S HOT...

Eco-chic. Live jazz. Beer in the evening.

WHAT'S NOT...

Leather 'n' lace. The jukebox. Whisky in the afternoon.

DAVID H WELLS »CORBIS

MOST BIZARRE SIGHT

The Visvesvaraya Industrial & Technical Museum, bordering Cubbon Park, showcases a mind-blowingly wacky collection of electrical and engineering contraptions, from a replica of the 1903 Wright Brothers aeroplane to virtual-reality gaming consoles.

CLASSIC RESTAURANT EXPERIENCE

No trip to Bengaluru is complete without a lunch stop at Koshy's Bar & Restaurant. A charmingly mothballed institution, Koshy's has played foster-home to Bengaluru's intelligentsia since 1952. Its coffee has inspired many a newspaper review, while scribbles for countless fine-art masterpieces have been executed on its supply of napkins. All of Bengaluru's newfangled restaurants together would never manage to undercut its old-world charm, or replicate its scrumptious fish 'n' chips platter, for that matter. Knock one back for nostalgia while you're here.

CLASSIC PLACE TO STAY

The grand dame of Bengaluru's heritage hotels, the Taj West End is rated among the top 10 luxury addresses in India. Dating from 1887, the hotel is also a botanist's delight – some 54 species of tropical flora flourish in its lush 20-acre garden. Its 19th-century villas and mansions, now renovated and outfitted with the most lavish creature comforts, have housed everyone from Sir David Lean to Mark Knopfler in the past.

EUROPE

◆ CÁDIZ

NORTH AMERICA

ASIA

AFRICA

'...the swashbuckling spirit has never quite left the city's veins and Cádiz remains a notorious party animal.'

by Oliver Smith

04 CÁDIZ, SPAIN

○ **POPULATION** 128,600

○ **FOREIGN VISITORS PER YEAR** 677,000

○ **LANGUAGE** SPANISH

○ **UNIT OF CURRENCY** EURO (€)

○ **COST INDEX** MIDRANGE DOUBLE HOTEL ROOM FROM €86 (US$123), TAPAS €2-4 (US$3-6), CLIMBING THE TOWERS OF OLD CÁDIZ €4 (US$6), ONE-WEEK SPANISH COURSE €185 (US$265)

WHY GO IN 2012? CARNIVAL CAPITAL

When it comes to swashbuckling cities, few can compete with Cádiz. This is a city whose fortune was made on the high seas – from the port of Cádiz, the Spanish navy ruled the Americas, returning from the New World laden with treasure that attracted the attention of dastardly pirates. Connected to the rest of Spain by a narrow strip of land, it doesn't seem impossible that Cádiz might yet follow in the footsteps of Christopher Columbus, and break off and set sail across the Atlantic.

This year, however, the Americas are coming to Cádiz. Though it's far closer to Morocco than Mexico, Cádiz has found itself named Ibero-American Capital of Culture for 2012 – the first time a European city has held the honour. Events are planned throughout the year, with art, music and performances from across Latin America being staged at venues across the town.

Fortunately, the swashbuckling spirit has never quite left the city's veins and Cádiz remains a notorious party animal. Admittedly, this might normally look like a peaceful pocket of old-world Spain, complete with old men in flat caps shuffling about in cafe-lined squares, and crumbling battlements standing beside shady parks. But once a year, sleepy Cádiz undergoes a Superman-like transformation and hosts Spain's most raucous carnival – a 10-day bender of drinking, singing and dancing, all conducted in fancy dress. The Gaditanos (residents of Cádiz) are famed throughout Spain for their wit, and this is put to the test during February's carnival.

ROBIN CHAPMAN »LPI

SPECTATOR SPORTS RULE AT CONIL DE LA FRONTERA

Wearing lipstick and neon wigs, groups perform satirical skits before discerning judges, with politicians, priests and public figures among the unfortunate souls who are mercilessly lampooned. If you find the official carnival proceedings a bit too straight-laced, join the ranks of the *ilegales* – groups of friends who assemble on the spur of the moment to compete with their (slightly) more organised counterparts.

LIFE-CHANGING EXPERIENCES

It may not pull the same crowds as Seville or Córdoba, but few places embody the spirit of gutsy Andalucían living like Cádiz. Try to pick up flamenco in the Barrio de Santa Maria, or brave the heights of the cathedral tower, Torre de Poniente, for views out over the rooftops of the old city, which is little changed since its glory days of the 17th century.

Alternatively, kick back in one of the cafes that line the Plaza San Juan de Dios and gorge on plates of fried fish, before digesting with a tentative paddle in the Atlantic at Playa de la Caleta – an urban beach guarded by sturdy fortifications.

FESTIVALS & EVENTS

✪ As if Cádiz needed any more excuses for merry making in 2012, the 19th of March marks the 200th anniversary of the first liberal Spanish constitution ('La Pepa'), which was proclaimed in the town. This document laid the foundations of modern Spanish state, so come prepared to party like a patriot.

4CORNERS IMAGES

○ July sees the Tall Ships Race arrive in Cádiz, with sailing boats from around the world anchoring in the harbour before setting sail for A Coruña in northern Spain.

○ Cádiz's answer to Halloween is 'Tosantos' – an All Saints Day feast on the 1st of November. This gastronomic showdown sees market stalls compete to sell the best fruit and charcuterie to hungry punters.

RANDOM FACTS

○ Cádiz could well be the oldest city still standing in Western Europe. Dating from the eighth century BC, legend tells that the town was founded by Hercules himself.

○ According to local folklore, the exotic plants in Cádiz's seafront parks are descended from souvenirs smuggled back from America by Christopher Columbus himself.

○ Locals were pleased when Cádiz was selected to play a starring role in the 2002 James Bond film *Die Another Day*. They were slightly less pleased to find their home town was 'playing' the Cuban capital of Havana.

CLASSIC PLACE TO STAY

A 19th-century townhouse hosts the Hotel Argantonio – perhaps the most charming place to stay in the old town of Cádiz. Arranged around a courtyard, there are plenty of reminders of the empires that have checked in over the centuries: French furnishings recall the Napoleonic wars, while ornate arches represent Cádiz's Moorish past.

○ STOCKHOLM

EUROPE

NORTH
AMERICA

ASIA

AFRICA

'…this is as seductive a capital city as can be imagined – cosy yet cosmopolitan, wilfully alternative and effortlessly picturesque.'

by Oliver Smith

05 STOCKHOLM, SWEDEN

○ **POPULATION** 2 MILLION

○ **FOREIGN VISITORS PER YEAR** 3.3 MILLION

○ **LANGUAGE** SWEDISH

○ **UNIT OF CURRENCY** SWEDISH KRONA (SEK)

○ **COST INDEX** DOUBLE ROOM AT THE LÅNGHOLMEN PRISON HOTEL 1590 SEK (US$255), CROSS-TOWN FERRY RIDE 40 SEK (US$6.25), ART GALLERY ADMISSION 100 SEK (US$16), STIEG LARSSON MILLENNIUM TOUR 120 SEK (US$18.45)

HOLGER LEUE » LPI

WHY GO IN 2012? THE MILLENNIUM BUG

Not so long ago, the world thought it had Stockholm figured out. It was, we thought, a Nordic paradise – a place where happy, healthy people roller-skated through tidy streets, where Nobel prizes were awarded, and where princes and princesses lived happily over after.

Then something happened – perhaps somebody put something in the water – because all of a sudden Stockholm lost its halo. The worldwide success of Stieg Larsson's Millennium trilogy turned Stockholm from a peaceful utopia to a sinister underworld of murderers, fraudsters and miscreants. Even the prince started dating a glamour model.

The film release of *The Girl with the Dragon Tattoo,* starring Daniel Craig as journalist Mikael Blomkvist, might have prompted a new wave of Stieg fans to look for the grimy side of Stockholm. Unfortunately they'll have to look quite hard, because Stockholm looks as perfect as it's ever been. From the winding cobbled alleyways of Gamla Stan to the pristine parks of Djurgården, this is as seductive a capital city as can be imagined – cosy yet cosmopolitan, wilfully alternative and effortlessly picturesque. Admittedly Stockholm has never been a cheap date; prices for accommodation and food can be shockingly high. But even if Stockholm leaves you with a lighter wallet, you'll inevitably still leave it with a heavy heart.

LIFE-CHANGING EXPERIENCES

Stockholm is set across a series of islands, each of which has its own particular way of doing things. Gamla Stan is the wise old grandpa of Stockholm's islands – amble down its medieval streets in the shadow of the royal palace, or hole up in one of its cafes. Skeppsholmen probably considers itself the most sophisticated of the islands, and here you can marvel at its Moderna Museet: a modern art collection housing pieces by Picasso, Matisse and Salvador Dalí.

With its trendy design shops and bohemian bars, the island of Södermalm is one of the coolest kids on the block, while the stately parks of Djurgården make it the best island for an evening stroll. Scattered to the east are the thousands of tiny islands that form the Stockholm archipelago – the city's favourite rustic weekend retreat.

FESTIVALS & EVENTS

✪ The Stockholm Furniture Fair on 7 February attracts big-name designers from Scandinavia and beyond. There's also a chance for members of the public to sneak in and ogle at the furniture (although flat-pack jokes won't be appreciated).

✪ The smooth grooves of July's Stockholm Jazz Festival in Skansen have been a summertime fixture for the best part of 30 years – previous performers have been as diverse as B.B. King and Missy Elliott.

✪ July marks the centenary of the 1912 Stockholm Olympics. The 14 July Jubilee marathon will retrace the route of the original event, arriving at the same finishing line.

JON HICKS »CORBIS

HOT TOPIC OF THE DAY

If you're getting bored with all the gushing over Prince William and his bride Kate Middleton, the Swedish royal family has proved a goldmine of gossip for Stockholmites in recent years. While dashing Prince Carl Philip has a passion for racing fast cars and has dated a reality TV star, the king himself has been rocked by allegations of an affair with a pop singer. Unfortunately, it's unlikely you'll bump into a misbehaving royal – they generally keep a discreet distance at the Drottningholm palace on the outskirts of the city.

MOST BIZARRE SIGHT

The Stockholm metro system lives a double life as Sweden's biggest art gallory, with sculptures, paintings and mosaics on display at stations across the network. Even the metro's architects got into the artistic spirit – the walls at Solna Centrum depict a spruce forest, while the ceilings at T-Centralen are elaborately patterned.

MOST UNUSUAL PLACE TO STAY

Stockholm has considerable pedigree when it comes to strange accommodation. Visitors can stay in the 'Jumbo' hostel (housed inside a Boeing 747 at Arlanda airport) or sleep aboard the *af Chapman* (a 19th-century sailing ship moored near the city centre). Neither, however, is quite as peculiar as the Långholmen Hotel – a once-notorious prison where guests can sleep in renovated cells.

○ GUIMARÃES

'The old city is a beguiling tangle of medieval, red-roofed, colonnaded buildings, punctuated by awe-inspiring mansions and palaces…'

by Abigail Hole

06 GUIMARÃES, PORTUGAL

❂ **POPULATION** 170,000

❂ **FOREIGN VISITORS PER YEAR** 100,000+

❂ **LANGUAGE** PORTUGUESE

❂ **UNIT OF CURRENCY** EURO (€)

❂ **COST INDEX** CUP OF WHITE COFFEE €0.90 (US$1.30), GLASS OF PORT €1 (US$1.40), MIDRANGE DOUBLE HOTEL ROOM €60-140 (US$85-200), SHORT TAXI RIDE €8 (US$11.50), CUSTARD TART €0.75 (US$1.10)

JAVIER LARREA » PHOTOLIBRARY

WHY GO IN 2012? IT'S A CULTURAL FEAST

Ever thought about going to Guimarães? If the answer is 'no', you'll hardly be alone. This northern Portugal city is breathtakingly beautiful, as recognised by its place on the Unesco World Heritage List, yet mysteriously it doesn't figure on the radars of many foreign visitors It certainly has historical clout: settled since the 9th century, it was central to the formation of the Portuguese state, and became the country's first capital city. It's also packed full of architectural riches; in fact, nothing much has changed architecturally within the city walls since the 15th century. The old city is a beguiling tangle of medieval, red-roofed, colonnaded buildings, punctuated by awe-inspiring mansions and palaces, and centred on a spikily crenellated castle. Yet Guimarães consistently gets overlooked in the rush to explore Lisbon, Coimbra, Porto and nearby Braga.

But now is the moment to visit, as the city celebrates its status as a cultural powerhouse, because it's been anointed the European Capital of Culture in 2012. Building on an already impressive cultural scene and fired up by its significantly youthful population, the city will be a hot spot of artistic endeavour throughout the year, with creative artists gathering from across Portugal and Europe to showcase their work in the areas of cinema, photography, fine arts, architecture, literature, philosophy, theatre, dance and street art. The calendar is crammed with cultural events, concerts, performances and festivals. In June the renovated neighbourhood of Nossa Senhora da Conceição will be launched with a celebratory performance featuring song and dance. The year of culture will culminate on 20 December with *Krisis* – a show created by the community and curated by cutting-edge Portuguese rock group Mão Morta.

LIFE-CHANGING EXPERIENCES

Visit the medieval castle, with its fierce battlements and skirt of green grass, before feeling dwarfed as you explore the 15th-century Palace of the Dukes of Bragança, a gracious and imposing stone symbol of the former power and prestige of the Bragança

STEFANO TORRIONE » PHOTOLIBRARY

EVEN THE VESPAS ARE OLD-SCHOOL HERE – PRAÇA DE SANTIAGO

family. Next, take a soaring ride on the town's novel cable car for inspirational views over the city and its surrounding countryside. Come the evening, visit Guimarães' Centro Cultural Vila Flor, an arts centre housed in an 18th-century palace and the heart of the city's burgeoning, youth-fired music and arts scene. It's a happening place that encompasses amphitheatres and the Café Concerto, all of which host regular gigs and performances.

FESTIVALS & EVENTS
✪ The ancient ritual of Clamor also celebrates its 400th year in the city in 2012. Popularly known as the 'Ronda da Lapinha', it's a grand religious procession between Lapinha and Guimarães that takes place annually on the third Sunday of June.

WHAT'S HOT...
Youth – over half the inhabitants of Guimarães are under 30 years old, making it one of the youngest populations in Europe.

WHAT'S NOT...
The euro. Inflation.

HOT TOPIC OF THE DAY
Has the Portuguese bail-out worked? How is the Portuguese economy faring? Is it recovering faster than Greece, Ireland or Spain? Is unemployment going to continue to rise? And if all that's too depressing, there's always the football.

MOST BIZARRE SIGHT
The Stone House attracts thousands of visitors every year. This seemingly Flintstones-built structure in the Montanhas de Fafe, a short trip 15km northeast of Guimarães, is a remotely set private house. It appears to have been constructed by hollowing out an enormous pebble (it's a structure built between four huge boulders), with slightly higgledy-piggledy windows, topped by an irregular red roof and a chimney. It's the most fairytale place imaginable – you expect either a wicked witch or a wizened wizard to appear at the door. Quite simply, it's one of the most curious buildings in the world.

CLASSIC PLACE TO STAY
Set on a hill overlooking the city is the majestic Pousada de Guimarães – Santa Marinha, a sprawling 12th-century Augustine convent that's been renovated into a midrange hotel. If you like palatial surroundings, gardens, hidden corners with granite fountains, rich Portuguese glazed tiles, cloisters, and balconies and terraces with sweeping views over the city, then you'll be happy here.

'Culture and sports have come to the fore…
Dining is now top-notch, nightlife exhilarating and
international luxury hotel chains are coming…'

○ SANTIAGO

by Carolyn McCarthy

07 SANTIAGO, CHILE

○ **POPULATION** 5.2 MILLION

○ **FOREIGN VISITORS PER YEAR** 939,000

○ **LANGUAGE** SPANISH

○ **UNIT OF CURRENCY** CHILEAN PESO

○ **COST INDEX** BOTTLE OF WINE 3800 PESOS (US$8), MIDRANGE DOUBLE
HOTEL ROOM 50,000 PESOS (US$107), SHORT TAXI RIDE 1800 PESOS (US$4),
HELISKIING AT VALLE NEVADO 99 PESOS (US$210)

WHY GO IN 2012? A SEISMIC SHIFT IS HAPPENING

Wedged between Andean peaks and Pacific rollers, Chile's insular and isolated geography once kept it lagging behind international fashions and cultural movements. As a capital city, Santiago was staid and starched, thanks partly to the intellectual and artistic exodus during the Pinochet years. Once the dictator was brought to account, however, business confidence returned, creating a granite stability that remains the envy of South America.

Travellers, alas, crave excitement and stimulation – no one wants to date stability and fewer want to send a postcard from there. But then calamity came calling to Chile, first through an 8.8-magnitude earthquake and later when 33 miners were trapped in the country's north. With the world watching, Chile displayed its defiant optimism in the face of adversity. These experiences have seemed to ignite a seismic shift in the capital. Culture and sports have come to the fore – suddenly everyone owns spandex and spends Saturdays pedalling the hairpin turns in the hills. New museums, including the Centro Cultural Gabriella Mistral and the Museo de la Moda, have opened to acclaim. Dining is now top-notch, nightlife exhilarating and international luxury hotel chains are coming to call (Santiago now boasts the first W Hotel in South America), while this year also marks the inauguration of the tallest building on the continent, the 70-storey Torre Gran Costanera, with a complex of offices, shops and restaurants. Visit Santiago in 2012 and you'll feel the buzz.

LIFE-CHANGING EXPERIENCES

One of the biggest attractions of Santiago is its surroundings. Day trippers can scale an Andean peak in summer, ski its powder-clad slopes in July, or cycle through the idyllic vineyards of the Casablanca, Maipo and Colchagua valleys. Scale down any of these activities and they're perfect for the family.

PERUSE, PONDER, PUZZLE – ART AT THE MUSEUM

In the city, hit the labyrinth of fruit and vegetable stalls at the grungy but gratifying market La Vega and chat with the vendors. Ditch the crowded Metro for a bike tour, taking to the city streets. Peruse the galleries, recaffeinate in a counter-culture cafe in Bellas Artes and dine in the Paris-style neighborhood of Lastarria or its hipster cousin, Bellavista.

FESTIVALS & EVENTS

✪ In January, Latin America's biggest theatre festival, Santiago a Mil (loosely translated as Santiago Rush), brings drama from cultural centres to the street, with international works, emerging theatre and acrobats.

✪ Chile rocks in April with the first international edition of Lollapalooza, with 60 bands playing Parque O'Higgins; kids can get their hair punked at the adjoining Kidsapalooza.

✪ Chilean Independence is feted at Fiestas Patrias (the week of 17 September), with a week of big barbecues, *terremotos* (a potent wine punch) and merry making.

RECENT FAD

A slick addition to the city, the W hotel in Plaza Peru is the city's hottest address. Just ask Jay Z and Beyonce, who slipped up to the rooftop bar for virgin strawberry mojitos.

WHAT'S HOT...

The new: hip-hop, omelettes, mountain biking and boutique breweries. The traditional: classic dive bars like La Piojera and the parody news of *The Clinic*. Spend time with both.

WHAT'S NOT...

Eighties fashion: feathered hairdos and slouchy boots. Café con Piernas: these historic coffee shops with bad coffee and semi-naked waitresses seem to have had their day.

HOT TOPIC OF THE DAY

While Santiago grows and prospers, its shrinking green space worries residents, who have put their weight behind a new urban reforestation program by adopting trees – the ultimate goal is one for every citizen.

MOST BIZARRE SIGHT

Tramping off an Andean glacier to find yourself beneath Santiago's skyscrapers within the space of a couple of hours simply boggles the mind.

CLASSIC PLACE TO STAY

Snug against Santiago's midcity mountain are Bellavista's stately mansions and leafy streets. Poet Pablo Neruda once lived here; now it's the heart of the city's tireless nightlife. For respite, turn to the Aubrey, a mission-style mansion with art deco touches. Guests praise the pampering, but having a heated pool under the palm trees is a nice touch, too.

HONG KONG

'…a particularly exciting year for Hong Kong, as it continues its march towards full democracy with a new model for its legislature.'

by Piera Chen

08 HONG KONG, CHINA

✪ **POPULATION** 7.1 MILLION

✪ **FOREIGN VISITORS PER YEAR** 36 MILLION

✪ **LANGUAGES** CANTONESE, ENGLISH

✪ **UNIT OF CURRENCY** HONG KONG DOLLAR (HK$)

✪ **PRICE PER SQ FT OF A HOME** $8000 (US$1,025) TO $80,000 (US$10,256)

✪ **COST INDEX** PINT OF TSINGTAO HK$48 (US$6), MIDRANGE DOUBLE HOTEL ROOM HK$900-4500 (US$115-578), DORM BED UK$180-750 (US$23-96), DIM SUM MEAL PER PERSON HK$40-300 (US$5-38), SHORT MTR RIDE HK$10 (US$1.25), ONE WAY/RETURN PEAK TRAM RIDE HK$28/40 (US$3.50/$5)

WHY GO IN 2012? HONG KONG OUT LOUD

The mood in China's most liberated city is edgier and more vocal than ever. In recent years it has experienced a flourishing protest culture, with greater numbers of young and middle-class citizens taking to the streets. Rallies are infused with theatrics and eruptions of song, dance and poetry, reflecting the city's vibrant indie music and literary scenes. This will be a particularly exciting year for Hong Kong, as it continues its march towards full democracy with a new model for its legislature – the new assembly will have the power to implement full public elections, so far an evasive ideal for the city's inhabitants. So is 2012 as good as it gets? Hong Kongers are not holding their breath, but they certainly dare to hope.

The city is also lending its voice to the past. You can kowtow to kung-fu heavyweight Bruce Lee, with an exhibition on the legendary fighter at the Heritage Museum, while celebrated film director King Hu *(A Touch of Zen)* gets his own retrospective at the Hong Kong Film Archive (both planned for 2012 at the time of writing). For some light relief, check out the antics of Ocean Park's newest guests, Arctic penguins.

RICHARD I'ANSON » LPI

GET SOME BRIGHT LIGHT THERAPY AT LUNAR NEW YEAR

LIFE-CHANGING EXPERIENCES

The classic Hong Kong experiences are still there to be sampled. Enjoy views of skyscrapers marching up hills from the Star Ferry, then take the funicular tram up to the Peak for more spectacular vistas, before challenging your senses at a wet market or divining your future at a temple. Go shopping, gallery hopping and check out the bars of Soho. Explore walled villages or go hiking on Asia's most breathtaking trails – Hong Kong is 70% rolling hills. Whatever you do, sprinkle your day generously and boldly with some of the city's 11,000 restaurants.

FESTIVALS & EVENTS

✪ The biggest event of the year is the Dragonboat Carnival (28 June to 1 July), where some 200 teams will churn up the waters of Victoria Harbour. The carnival includes the Club Crew World Championships, which returns here in 2012 for the first time since the birth of modern dragonboat racing in the city, 36 years ago.

✪ During the Mid-Autumn Festival (29 September to 1 October), a 70m 'dragon' aglow with thousands of incense sticks pinned to its body snakes its way through Tai Hang.

✪ The month-long Hong Kong Photo Festival starting in October features works by worthy photographers from Hong Kong and East Asia.

MOST BIZARRE SIGHT

Under the Canal Rd Flyover, you can hire old ladies to beat up your enemy. Well, symbolically. From their perch on plastic stools, these rent-a-curse grannies will pound paper cut-outs of that love rival, office bully or whiny celeb with a shoe (your Adidas or their orthopedic flat – your call) while rapping curses. A practice related to folk sorcery, villain hitting is said to bring reconciliation, though that, too, is likely to be symbolic.

CLASSIC RESTAURANT EXPERIENCE

If you can only dine once in Hong Kong, do so at Luk Yu. Its (Michelin-lauded) Cantonese fare alone is worth a trip. But this elegant teahouse (c 1933) in eastern art deco style was also the haunt of famous Chinese opera artists, writers, newspaper publishers and painters. These tousled glamorati held soirées, gave recitals and discussed the national fate over baskets of steaming dim sum. Today, under the ceiling fans and stained-glass windows, waiters will pour your tea in that pleasantly irreverent manner that came to be associated with the place.

BEST SHOPPING

Between them, Tsim Sha Tsui and Causeway Bay have all the wearables you'll want for life. Hollywood Rd with its art and antiques meet loftier needs, while Sham Shui Po ensures a jostle with the locals over electronic gadgets. For the ultimate, retro-with-a-twist Hong Kong souvenir, visit G.O.D.

WILL ROBB » LPI

EUROPE

NORTH
AMERICA

ASIA

✪ ORLANDO

AFRICA

AUSTRALIA

'the 61st NBA All-Star Weekend…the hippest sporting event in the USA, it brings much of the basketball and music worlds together'

by Robert Reid

09 ORLANDO, FLORIDA

✪ **POPULATION** 2.1 MILLION

✪ **FOREIGN VISITORS PER YEAR** 3.3 MILLION

✪ **VISITORS TO DISNEY WORLD'S MAGIC KINGDOM PER YEAR** 17 MILLION

✪ **LANGUAGE** ENGLISH

✪ **UNIT OF CURRENCY** US DOLLAR (US$)

✪ **COST INDEX** CUP OF COFFEE US$2, MIDRANGE DOUBLE HOTEL ROOM US$94, TAXI RIDE FROM AIRPORT TO THEME PARKS US$55, ONE-DAY PASS TO DISNEY WORLD US$87, SEEING JACK KEROUAC'S HOUSE FREE

RANDY FARIS »PHOTOLIBRARY

WHY GO IN 2012? THE CITY ITSELF

That's right – oft-neglected Orlando. Away from the theme parks, the city itself is surprisingly inviting. Built on a bedrock of limestone pocked with little lakes, it features leafy blocks with Cracker-style mid-century homes you could imagine yourself living in. And historical leafy 'hoods, like Thorntroo Park or College Park, boast B&Bs, boutique eateries and shops, a gorgeous museum complex and some of the best Vietnamese food outside Saigon. Greater Orlando hopes to attract 50 million visitors this year, but most will head for the parks and miss out on the city itself. But it's time all that changed.

This should be a great year for Orlando as it's hosting the 61st NBA All-Star Weekend (25 and 26 February). Don't laugh – this is a big deal. The hippest sporting event in the USA, it brings much of the basketball and music worlds together for slam-dunk contests, after-hours parties and concerts, as well as the all-star game itself.

It's worth poking around the city, too. Keep an eye on the boho 'Milk District', a neighbourhood on the rise with its motley crew of eateries, bars serving microbrews, bookshops and tattoo parlours, just a short drive east of downtown. Orlando, hip? Who knew?

LIFE-CHANGING EXPERIENCES

Yes, you have to go to a theme park. Disney World is the biggest on earth, but Universal's Simpsons ride is still our favourite of all time – for sheer imagination and humour, and an upset stomach afterwards. Back in town, the big change is just going to town. Start at the museum complex at Loch Haven Park – surrounded by water, it's a stunner. But the best is the Mennello Museum of Art, featuring local Earl Cunningham's unforgettable self-trained works: paint on glass, with oversized animals and very tiny people.

FESTIVALS & EVENTS

✪ All March, baseball fans can see watch the Atlanta Braves' spring training games at the nearby town of Lake Buena Vista.

✪ Downtown's buzzy, three-day Florida Music Festival turns 10 in April 2012. It's huge,

NORBERT EISELE-HEIN » IMAGEBROKER

YES, YOU HAVE TO GO TO A THEME PARK – IN THIS CASE, DISCOVERY COVE

with 250 big-name and unsigned bands (don't scoff at the latter; Taylor Swift played here before hitting it big). A three-day pass is just $25.

✪ April's Fiesta Medina, one of Central Florida's premier Latin American festivals, turns 25 this year, with tens of thousands coming for a one-day explosion of live music, food, dance and family friendly mayhem.

✪ From mid-May to mid-June it's *Star Wars* central, when Disney's Hollywood Studios hosts '*Star Wars* Weekends' where you can meet 50 *Star Wars* characters.

RECENT FAD

The newest Orlando park-goer wears cute little crimson-and-gold ties, black robes and sometimes lightning-bolt face paint. That's right, Potter Pilgrims. Since opening in June 2010, Universal Studio's Wizarding World of Harry Potter – actually just a part of its Islands of Adventure – has proved hugely popular, especially for its Forbidden Journey ride in Hogwarts Castle. Only die-hards don't throw out the $11 butter beer.

HOT TOPIC OF THE DAY

High-speed rail projects. President Obama set aside funds for a new Tampa–Orlando link, but the state government nixed it.

RANDOM FACTS

✪ The town was originally called Jernigan before it became Orlando. No one's exactly sure why, but the most likely culprit is a soldier named Orlando Reeves, who may or may not have died near Lake Eola.

✪ Musically, Orlando bands can get a bit sappy. Matchbox 20, NSync and Backstreet Boys? All Orlandoians.

✪ Disney World's not technically in Orlando.

MOST BIZARRE SIGHT

Jack Kerouac's house is in Orlando? It's hard to imagine, but after writing *On the Road,* the Beat Generation legend moved to 1418 Clouser Ave, and lived in a quaint Cracker-style home under a giant oak sprouting Spanish moss in family-friendly College Park... with his mum. Equally oddly, Kerouac typed out his counter-culture *Dharma Bums* in this *Leave It to Beaver*–style neighbourhood. The house is now part of the Keroauc Project, a writer-in-residence program.

CLASSIC RESTAURANT EXPERIENCE

Orlando has some of the country's finest, most authentic and best-value Vietnamese food. Don't leave without trying one of the many restaurants in 'ViMi' or 'Little Saigon', centred on Mills Ave and Colonial Dr, not far northeast of downtown. A great, cheap choice is Little Saigon Restaurant.

> 'Multicultural, freewheeling and vibrant, it's now a hip city to visit rather than just the end of the road for lost souls.'

✪ DARWIN

by Meg Worby

10 DARWIN, AUSTRALIA

✪ **POPULATION** 124,800

✪ **FOREIGN VISITORS PER YEAR** 157,200

✪ **LANGUAGE** ENGLISH

✪ **UNIT OF CURRENCY** AUSTRALIAN DOLLAR (AU$)

✪ **COST INDEX:** STUBBIE OF BEER A$7 (US$7.30), CUP OF COFFEE $AU4.50 (US$4.70), MIDRANGE HOTEL DOUBLE ROOM A$100-200 (US$104-208), DORM BED A$24-33 (US$25-34.30), ENTRY TO KAKADU NATIONAL PARK A$25 (US$26)

ANDREW WATSON »LPI

WHY GO 2012? TRIP THE TOP-END FANTASTIC

It was once easy to dismiss Darwin as a frontier town full of brawling fishermen, dreamy hippies and redneck truckers. Raggedy and transient, it's always been a place to lose yourself, find yourself or reinvent yourself – the kind of place that attracts people who don't fit in anywhere else. But all that is changing. With a pumping nocturnal scene, magical markets and restaurants, and world-class wilderness areas just down the road, today Darwin is the triumph of Australia's Top End. Multicultural, freewheeling and vibrant, it's now a hip city to visit rather than just the end of the road for lost souls.

And now is the time to go. Beat the crowds to the redeveloping Waterfront Precinct with its wave pool, bars and wharf eateries; or score some brilliant Indigenous art before East Coast galleries snap it up and charge double. When southern Australia is chilling through winter, here it's blue skies, party nights and sleeping late. It's also a hot-ticket backpacker destination: Mitchell St after dark is hormones, hedonism and a whole lotta fun.

LIFE-CHANGING EXPERIENCES

Change down a gear to Top End time. Nose your way through the food stalls at Mindil Beach Sunset Market, then watch the sun melt into the Timor Sea. Saturday morning's Parap Village Market is a low-key, smoky den of Southeast Asian cooking carts, fresh-cut jungle flowers and fragrant fruits. Take in a movie at the outdoor Deckchair Cinema, then linger over a few cold ones at a street-side bar on Mitchell St. Swing by the outstanding Museum & Art Gallery of the Northern Territory, or lose yourself in the rampant wilds of Kakadu, Litchfield and Nitmiluk national parks – just a few hours down the track.

FESTIVALS & EVENTS

✪ Coinciding with the fab Tiwi Art Sale, the Tiwi Islands Grand Final kicks off at the end of March on Bathurst Island. This is Aussie Rules football at its passionate, free-flowing best. Thousands jump on the ferry or fly over from Darwin for the day.
✪ In June the Darwin Blues Festival fires-up the Darwin Ski Club (water, not snow) with much boozing and bendy guitar strings.
✪ The Beer Can Regatta at Mindil Beach in July features races for boats constructed from 'tinnies' (help the locals empty a few for next year's race).
✪ Every August the Darwin Aboriginal Art Fair is a two-day art feast showcasing the talents of regional Indigenous artists.

WHAT'S HOT...

Satay prawns at Mindil Beach Sunset Market. Darwin's Waterfront Precinct. Indigenous artist Harold Thomas (designer of Australia's distinctive Aboriginal flag).

WHAT'S NOT...

Dorms with no air-con. Getting caught in monsoonal rain. Over-boozed backpackers.

JAMES BRAUND » LPI

MOST BIZARRE SIGHT

Pride of place among the stuffed species at the Museum & Art Gallery of the Northern Territory undoubtedly goes to 'Sweetheart': a 5m-long, 780kg saltwater crocodile. He met his maker in 1979 after terrorising fishermen on the Finniss River south of Darwin, attacking several boats over a five-year period.

CLASSIC RESTAURANT EXPERIENCE

Hanuman on Mitchell St is an airy, mod-Asian food room with just enough style to make it feel hip without any dress-code dramas (you can wear a T-shirt). Give your libido a nudge with some oysters in lemon grass, chilli and coriander, washed down with a killer Long Island Iced Tea.

BEST SHOPPING

Forget shiny lacquered boomerangs – for an authentic Top End souvenir check out Darwin's superb Indigenous art galleries. Local Aboriginal artists produce gorgeous fibre sculptures, weavings and paintings. Buying from a reputable gallery will ensure that your money actually makes it back to the artist; try Mbantua Fine Art Gallery or Territory Colours, both on Smith St Mall.

MOST UNUSUAL PLACE TO STAY

Spend the night at Feathers Sanctuary, in a beautifully designed 'Bali meets bush' timber-and-iron cottage with open-air bathroom and luxe interiors. Explore the lush gardens and waterhole, home to more tropical birds than you're likely to see in one place again. Gangly brolgas dance at dusk and sleek jabirus (Australia's only stork species) steal the show.

136
**BEST-VALUE
DESTINATIONS
FOR 2012**

140
**THE 10 BEST
THINGS TO DO
IN 2012**

144
**TOP SPOTS TO
WITNESS THE
APOCALYPSE**

148
**TOP 10 PLACES
TO PUT
YOURSELF IN
THE PICTURE**

152
**TOP SPOTS TO
GLAMP**

176
**THE WORLD'S
FINEST FREEBIES**

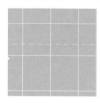

180
**BEST PLACES
FOR INTREPID
ROMANTICS**

184
**BEST PLACES TO
FIND MIDDLE
EARTH**

188
**GREATEST RACES
TO WATCH LIVE**

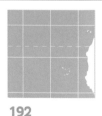

192
**TOP 007
DESTINATIONS**

BEST-VALUE DESTINATIONS FOR 2012

IF PAST YEARS (OR RECESSIONS) HAVE SUCKED UP YOUR TRAVEL BUDGET, PLAN SMART AND GET MORE BANG FOR YOUR BUCK IN 2012.

MARTIN MOOS » LPI

01 NORTHEASTERN USA

Cities of the American northeast – New York, Boston and Washington DC – might not be the world's cheapest, but you can save a bundle by taking advantage of the recent boom of budget bus companies. These buses, which also connect with Philadelphia, Toronto, Pittsburgh and even Charlotte, are a steal at about US$5 one way (and sometimes just US$1). Considering most destinations are ped-friendly (with good public transport and walkable centres), you can hop-scotch across the region without booking a flight or hiring a car. Better still, the ride's comfortable, there's free wi-fi, buses leave on time and there's often plenty of room.

Book early online for serious discounts on cheap routes at Megabus (www.megabus .com) and BoltBus (www.boltbus.com).

02 TAJIKISTAN

Marco Polo was impressed, and you will be too, once you experience the stunning scenery of this safe, stable Central Asian nation. It can be accessed at dirt cheap rates, even including the hire of a car and driver. Getting a Russian Lada for several days can be arranged for about US$300, which opens up the Afghan border and Pamir Highway, one of the world's greatest road trips. You'll stop off at hot springs, 2000-year-old stone structures and cartoon-style forts, finishing your days at village homestays or yurts for about US$10 per person. For even less, make a DIY trek to emerald lakes close to the Uzbek border.

Murgab Ecotourism Association has community-based yurtstays for US$5-$10 per person. See http://phiproject.free.fr.

03 LESOTHO

Mountains, cannibal caves, dinosaur footprints, crafts markets – and you get around by pony. Welcome to Lesotho, the 'kingdom of the sky'. Completely enveloped by South Africa, it's a cheaper proposition than its powerful neighbour, with pony treks its main tourist drawcard. The best deals are to the west at off-the-beaten-track Malealea, about 60km southeast of the capital Masuru, where multiday treks lead into a massive mountain range and landscape coloured musk and orange. It's extraordinary – and cheaper than pony treks in the east. Overnight trips, including a pony, food and a guide, begin at US$50 per day.

Malealea Lodge (www.malealea.co.ls) is a century-old trading post transformed into a well-run lodge with pony treks and good meals.

✪ MEKONG DELTA, VIETNAM

Vietnam is always good value, but you can now skip the package trips arranged in Ho Chi Minh City that tread the same worn-out routes. It's become easier, more rewarding and just as cheap to go on DIY multiday adventures to destinations like Ben Tre, Chao Doc and the floating markets of Vinh Long, and some less-seen ones like Ha Tien or Tra Vinh. Go by air-conditioned bus or hire moto-taxis as you go; the latter know ferry crossings on roads not on any map. Boat trips go for US$5 to US$10, while most guesthouses range from US$10 to US$25.

Take a ferry or plane from Rach Gia to the beaches of Phu Quoc Island, then fly back to Ho Chi Minh City. Short flights are cheap – under US$50.

❂ SAN FRANCISCO, USA

The city by the bay might be expensive to live in, but it practically begs you to visit. Little boutique hotels near Union Sq can be had for under US$100 – a fraction of what you'll pay in New York or London. Beyond the street cars (the historic ones on Market St are cheaper than the touristy cable cars), BART has cheap, easy links to San Francisco's airport – no need for US$60 taxi rides. Food-wise, San Francisco's 'mission burrito' (stuffed with rice, beans and *carne asada*) goes for US$5 in the bar-filled Mission. And there's so much cheap and free stuff to do: walking the Golden Gate, Pacific beaches, vintage arcade Musée Mécanique and a host of free galleries.

Check out the Diego Rivera Gallery (www.sfai.edu), featuring a 1931 trompe l'oeil mural.

❂ JAPAN

Japan had a rough 2011, with the March earthquake and a hard year for tourism, so travelling there is not only a good thing to do, but can make financial sense. Compared with London, Paris or New York, its attractions and accommodation are often much cheaper. In Tokyo simple, Japanese-style *minshuku* guesthouses run from j3000 (US$37). Also, many attractions are free (eg temples, botanic gardens) or cheap (the Tokyo National Museum is a fifth the cost of Tower of London); some, like the Nagano ski runs or Disney tickets, are cheaper than Alps lift tickets or Mickey Mouse's entry in Anaheim.

The International Tourism Centre for Japan (www.itcj.jp) lists excellent-value minshuku guesthouses.

❂ OHRID, MACEDONIA

There's always a race for the next big thing in Europe, and budget-friendly Macedonia is rising in popularity for its mountainous setting of vineyards, lakes and Byzantine churches; it's also a mainstay stop-off on Balkan trips. Beyond the lively capital Skopje, the spiritual heart is three road hours' west at Ohrid, a lovely town with a medieval castle looking over church-lined hilly streets and the lush coastline of Lake Ohrid. Private rooms are easy to find for €10 euro or less, while opulent historic villas turned into B&Bs run for under €50 (US$71.50). Bus services run to sites along the lake coast, including Galičica National Park with hiking, boating and swimming spots.

For info on local services, contact Lost in Ohrid (www.lostinohrid.com).

❂ MÉRIDA, MEXICO

Most equate the Yucatan with beaches, but the best place to experience the food, life and architecture of the 'real Mexico' is a few hours inland at this lively city. Historic homes have been turned into inns, often for a fraction of the cost of Cancún resorts. The Spanish colonial centre of Plaza Grande has 16th-century cathedrals and free art museums; on weekends it hosts dance, food and parties. Day trips to five Mayan sites on the public Ruta Puuc bus loop go for about US$40, or head to the village of Celestún and hire a motorboat (US$17 per person) to see hundreds of pink flamingos in the mangroves.

Mérida's guesthouses are a bargain; rooms at Hotel Trinidad start at US$21 (www.hotelestrinidad.com).

✪ IQUITOS, PERU

Booking a five-day Amazon cruise from abroad can run to US$3500 per person, not including flights. That can be cut at least in half by dealing directly with folks in Iquitos – the world's biggest city not reachable by road. Local outfits can tailor trips to venture into piranha fishing spots, look for pink dolphins in the wildlife-rich Allpahuayo Mishana National Reserve (stopping at native villages to mingle with Amazonians) or reach the rustic Otorongo Lodge on the Colombian border. Meanwhile, Iquitos is interesting in itself: Eiffel (of Eiffel Tower) fame came to build rubber baron's mansions. The best time to visit is October or November, when it's still dry but before summer crowds.

For examples of trips on offer, check out Dawn on the Amazon (www.dawnontheamazon.com).

✪ PORTO, PORTUGAL

The town that put the 'Port' in Portugal (as well as the port in your wine glass) is a seriously good deal. Connected with much of Europe via budget airlines, Porto is a lovely town of atmospheric narrow lanes, village-like plazas and buildings decked in azuelo tile. You can stay in antique-filled inns with river views from just €25 (US$37.75), take a ride on an historical tram (€1; US$1.40) or head to the beach near Afurada village by ferry (€1). A few hours east is the traditional wine district of Alto Douro, where you cruise in a flat-bottomed boat (€20; US$28.50) and sleep in 200-year-old homes (€60; US$86). And did we mention the port?

The Ribeira district has dozens of lodges offering cheap wine tastings and tours (eg Vinologia; www.lamaisondesporto.com).

DJ JONES » LPI

RED HOT POKERS WILL LIGHT YOUR WAY TO RIBANENG WATERFALLS, LESOTHO

THE 10 BEST
THINGS TO DO
IN 2012

ANNIVERSARIES, GLOBAL GATHERINGS AND ESSENTIAL
DESTINATIONS FOR THE YEAR – 2012 TRAVEL PLANNING STARTS HERE

01 HONOUR SCOTT'S POLAR CENTENARY

British explorer Robert Falcon Scott's expedition to the South Pole arrived on 17 January 1912, by which point they already knew they were beaten by Amundsen's triumph on 14 December 1911. A century later, the Antarctic summer of 2011–12 will be a bumper one for visits to the frozen continent, which will have to be booked months in advance. Scott buffs should aim for Cambridge, England (home to the Polar Museum, part of the Scott Polar Research Institute) or his statue in London's Waterloo Place. But the ultimate is to visit his frozen-in-time hut at Cape Evans on Ross Island, Antarctica. Start saving those pennies.
The Scott Centenary concert tour featuring the City of London Sinfonia will tour England in February. See www.spri.cam .ac.uk/museum/exhibitions for details.

02 FOLLOW NAPOLEON ACROSS RUSSIA

Da da da da da da da da, daa daaa...BOOM! (That's Tchaikovsky's *1812 Overture*, complete with cannon fire.) Yes, this year marks the 200th anniversary of 1812 – and Napoleon's disastrous invasion of Russia and the battles provoked by it. Head to Moscow, where the Battle of Borodino Panorama gives a vivid impression of the events of a key skirmish. Or go further north to St Petersburg's Hermitage and Museum of Artillery, Engineers and Signal Corps, which contain paintings and memorabilia from the campaign. This could also be the year to finally tackle Tolstoy's epic *War and Peace,* set around the conflict – though you may need to set aside the entire year to get through it.
The 360-degree panorama of the Borodino battle – complete with sound effects – is at Kutuzovsky pr 38, Moscow.

03 VISIT NAMIBIA'S PROTECTED COAST

Namibia is a special country, blessed with an abundance of easy-to-spot wildlife, beautiful desert scenery and vast, wide-open spaces. This year you can visit the epic Namibian coastline in the knowledge that the entire Atlantic shore is now part of one of the world's largest protected areas, encompassing four parks: the Sperregebiet National Park, Namib Naukluft Park, newly created Dorob National Park and the infamous Skeleton

RALPH HOPKINS » LPI

Coast protected area. Many areas, especially in the south, can be explored independently – though ideally with your own wheels – but getting into serious Skeleton Coast wilderness requires a charter flight and deep pockets.

Chameleon Safaris (www.chameleonsafaris com) offers good-value safaris across Namibia, including the Skeleton Coast

✪ GO FOOTBALL CRAZY IN POLAND & UKRAINE

This summer's European Football Championship shines a light on two of Europe's least appreciated destinations. Poland and Ukraine are providing four venues each, and the rewards for travelling fans are set to be huge. Warsaw, Gdansk, Poznan and Wroclaw, Poland's host cities, frame a journey around that country, and you can tick off Krakow on the way to Europe's best-kept secret, Lviv in Ukraine. Kiev, which is especially lovely in the summer, Kharkiv and football-mad Donetsk complete the set of Ukrainian host venues (also see p8). Both countries offer some of the best-value travel in Europe, with easy transport links to ferry the continent's supporters to and from matches.

Get details about the venues and travel at www.uefa.com/uefaeuro2012/hostcountries.

✪ CHASE AUSTRALIA'S TOP END ECLIPSE

Eclipse chasers have had a bountiful few years, pairing one of nature's greatest shows with visits to Easter Island, Bhutan and Mongolia. This year's total eclipse on 13 November crosses parts of the South Pacific, with the most significant landfall across Arnhem Land and Cape

KARL LEHMANN » LPI

York in Australia's Northern Territory and Queensland, respectively. This is wild territory, and access to many areas is restricted by both permit requirements and wet season transport difficulties. However, the remote Palmer River area, inland from Port Douglas, Queensland, sees less rainfall than coastal areas and looks set to be a key eclipse-chasers destination. *Camping, facilities and a gold rush museum are available at the Palmer River Roadhouse on the Mulligan Hwy.*

✪ MEET THE MAID OF ORLEANS ON HER 600TH BIRTHDAY

France's greatest heroine was born 600 years ago this year, offering a great excuse to explore her former stamping ground. Joan of Arc was a teenage visionary and military hero who took the fight to the English in the Hundred Years War. Following her trail will lead travellers to some wonderful parts of France, from Orleans, where her boldness led to the lifting of a long siege, to the beautiful Reims Cathedral, where Charles VII was crowned King of France, having been inspired by her visions of his succession. Joan was tried in Rouen Castle and executed in the city's Vieux Marche, where a modern church marks the location of her immolation. *In preparation, read Mark Twain's fictional but illuminating Personal Recollections of Joan of Arc.*

✪ DISCOVER A NEW MIDDLE EAST

The Arab Spring swept through the region in 2011, offering revolutions that were variously realised or repressed. Few countries in the Middle East and North Africa were unaffected, but the most significant change may be in Western perceptions of the region. Despite their dubious political systems, these countries are steeped in history and offer hospitality unrivalled anywhere else; they're also are home to a young, energetic and ambitious population. Why not pay a visit to Tunis or Cairo – or any of the other cities that hit the headlines in 2011? You might be among the first to return, and you'll definitely be warmly welcomed.

Keep an eye on the headlines for the opening date of the amazing new Grand Egyptian Museum in Cairo, projected for some time in 2012.

✪ EXPLORE MARIBOR'S OLD TOWN

Sharing the European Capital of Culture crown with Guimarães, Portugal (p114) is the unheralded Slovenian gem of Maribor. The plan is to use the year in the spotlight to increase the profile of Slovenia's second-largest city, which is off the usual Ljubljana–Lake Bled–Triglav route through the country. Events are still being confirmed, but expect art, music and other festivals to accompany the well-established theatre, classical music and folklore performances. The real stars of the show will be Maribor's delightful Old Town and imposing castle, combined with a laid-back air best sampled from a cafe in one of the city's many delightful, diminutive squares.

Štajerc, a pub-restaurant at Vetrinjska ulica 30, is the place to head for if you're in the mood for reasonably priced local dishes.

✪ PLAY ARCADE CLASSICS AT THE SMITHSONIAN

Parents, kids, geeks and gamers should rejoice and head for the US capital. The collection at DC's Smithsonian American Art Museum has over 7000 works of art, but an exhibition this year proves this is no mere load of frames gathering dust. *The Art of Video Games* explores the evolution of arcade and computer games over 40 years, and promises to make almost everyone who visits feel nostalgic (and possibly ancient). Some 80 games will be featured through still images and video footage. Better yet, you warm up your fingers and then play Pac-Man, Super Mario Brothers, The Secret of Monkey Island, Myst and World of Warcraft.

The exhibition will run from 16 March to 30 September. See http://americanart.si.edu/ exhibitions.

✪ CHECK OUT KOREA'S EXPO

Today's descendants of World's Fairs, expos are large public exhibitions organised around a particular theme and featuring stands representing individual countries (think World Showcase at Disney World's Epcot Centre). The modern versions fascinate as much for the ways that countries strive to portray themselves as for the exhibits themselves. Yeosu in Korea is staging EXPO 2012, with a theme of 'Living Ocean and Coast', and the port city is a fitting venue with its spectacular coastline. Inside the Expo, expect thought-provoking, futuristic displays and dramatically designed pavilions.

Expo 2012 will be held from 12 May to 12 August.

TOP SPOTS TO
WITNESS THE APOCALYPSE

IT'S COMING ON 21 DECEMBER, ACCORDING TO MAYAN PROPHECIES. USHER IN THE BIG DAY AT THESE BUNKERS, RESORTS AND AUSPICIOUS SITES.

01 GREENBRIER RESORT, WEST VIRGINIA, USA

The Greenbrier's four golf courses, spring-fed spa and luxury suites have pampered 26 presidents – reason enough to book a room. Factor in the nuclear bunker and you've hit upon the perfect place for an end-of-world splurge. The US government built the underground facility in 1958 to house Congress in case of a Cold War attack. Agents worked undercover as hotel staff to ensure the 25-ton blast door, power plant, hospital and 1100 beds were ever-ready for action. While the covert project ceased operation in 1992, it's nice to know that a decontamination shower is there if you need it.

Public tours (US$30) of the bunker take place daily; rooms start at US$300 (www.greenbrier.com).

02 SEDONA, ARIZONA, USA

Does doomsday have you feeling stressed and unconnected? The vortexes of Sedona can remedy the problem. Native Americans have long deemed the landscape's red-rock buttes a hot spot where the earth's energy concentrates and radiates well-being. New Age advocates agree, having flocked here after the 'harmonic convergence' in 1987 to tap Sedona's mystical powers. Hike around the hills to feel the mojo, or get your aura read in the groovy town. Even if you don't believe the lore, it's a metaphysical moment come sunset, when the crimson rocks create an ethereal glow.

Earth Wisdom Jeep Tours (www.earthwisdomtours.com) take off into the scenic backcountry to explore the vortexes.

03 MOUNT ARARAT, EASTERN TURKEY

For a track record of staying dry in world-ending floods, look no further than Turkey's highest mountain. The 5200m peak is where Noah landed after God wiped out the planet with 40 days of rain, according to the famous Old Testament story that relates how Noah built an ark and set sail with two of every creature on earth. Evangelical explorers continue to 'find' the ark at various locations around the mountainside, though no claims have proved substantive so far. No matter – Mt Ararat is really all about sublime trekking... and the knowledge if the deluge comes, you're in a providential spot.

Outfitters such as Anatolian Adventures (www.anatolianadventures.com) arrange five-day treks starting at €375 (US$540).

✪ CHICHÉN ITZÁ, YUCATÁN, MEXICO

The Mayans are the ones who conceived the infamous 2012 date, so why not take a front-row seat at Chichén Itzá, their most spectacular ruins? The centrepiece of the 1500-year-old temple-city is El Castillo, aka the Pyramid of Kukulcán (the plumed serpent). The Mayans built it with 365 steps to represent the days of the year, and aligned it so during the spring and autumn equinox, the sun creates a light-and-shadow illusion of a snake descending the stairs. Debate the 2012 timetable all you want, but one thing's for sure: these folks sure knew their calendar.

Chichén Itzá is open from 8am to 5pm daily; www.visitmexico.com has details.

TIM BARKER » LPI

LOOK UP TO MT ARARAT, TURKEY'S HIGHEST MOUNTAIN, FROM ISHAK PASA SARAYI

✪ GLOBAL SEED VAULT, SVALBARD ISLANDS, NORWAY

Sunk deep into the permafrost 1300km from the North Pole, the Svalbard vault stores the planet's most precious kernels. It may sound like science fiction, but the underground chamber – designed to hold 4.5 million different seeds – is real; it opened in 2008 with a mission to preserve the genetic diversity of the world's food crops. Builders chose the remote location because it's safe from rising seas, seismic activity and other natural disasters, making it a fine place to hole up in uncertain times (though it gets a bit chilly, given the –18°C temperature inside).

See what plant species have been pre-served so far at www.nordgen.org/sgsv.

✪ ULURU, NORTHERN TERRITORY, AUSTRALIA

Uluru, aka Ayers Rock, rises up in Australia's red centre, a sandstone monolith of deep spiritual significance to the Anangu Aboriginal peoples. It's hard to explain everything it stands for, but think of it as the past, present and future wrapped into one, or as a blueprint for the world. Like Sedona, Uluru is considered one of the earth's power points, where many visitors experience a feeling of peace. The Anangu say the mighty stone has always existed – it just is – so there's no reason to think the end of days will impact it any differently.

Uluru-Kata Tjuta National Park (www.environment.gov.au/parks/uluru) is open year-round; admission is A425 (US$26).

✪ CAPITOL VISITOR CENTER, WASHINGTON DC, USA

An urban legend has developed around the subterranean visitor centre, which opened in 2008 beneath the US Capitol. Architects say they built it three storeys underground to preserve the white-domed landmark's historic views. They maintain the restricted third level was always earmarked for Congress' private use, and the $350 million-plus cost overruns were just politics as usual. Conspiracy theorists claim the off-limits area has been decked out as a bunker to protect Congress should catastrophe come knocking. Visitors can try to ascertain the truth during House and Senate tours, which start at the venue.

The centre is open 8.30am to 4.30pm Monday to Saturday, and admission is free; for trip planning see www.visitthecapitol.gov.

✪ GREAT PYRAMID, GIZA, EGYPT

Thanks to the film *StarGate,* you know the hulking Pyramid of Khufu is more than just a king's burial chamber – it's a portal to another planet! How else can one explain the mysterious passages leading from the tomb toward the sky (teleporters, duh) and the ancient structure's architectural precision (built by space beings with advanced skills, of course)? If this world is indeed ending in 2012, it will be prudent to be here, by the door to a new universe. And should the sci-fi turn out to be hooey, at least you've ticked one of the seven wonders of the world off the to-do list.

The Giza monuments, including the Sphinx, loom 25km from downtown Cairo; check www.lonelyplanet.com/egypt for the latest travel advisories.

✪ VIVOS SHELTER, NEBRASKA, USA

'It wasn't raining when Noah built the ark' is the tagline for this luxury bunker developer. Investors can buy a suite that will withstand everything from killer comets and chemical warfare to super-volcano eruptions. What's more, each of the 228 units comes equipped with carpeting, decorative artwork and access to the community wine cellar. Add in the DNA storage bank, armoured vehicle garage and a year's supply of freeze-dried spaghetti and pancake mix, and you have a heck of a doomsday hideaway. Vivos is located 70 miles from Omaha, though only shareholders know the exact location.

Bunkers cost US$25,000 per person; details on purchasing are at www.terravivos.com.

✪ GLASTONBURY TOR, ENGLAND

Whether it's the gateway to the Fairy Kingdom, the burial ground of the Holy Grail or the site of the enchanted Isle of Avalon, there's a whole lot of magic associated with this holy hill. It's said that King Arthur rests here, ready to wield his magical sword and help his country when it needs him most – for which the apocalypse will surely qualify. In the meantime, the modern town of Glastonbury is a great place to buy crystals, consult with psychics or lick vegan ice cream cones while waiting for the day of reckoning.

The tor is free to visit; arrange a B&B or nearby farm-stay at www.visitsomerset .co.uk.

TOP 10 PLACES TO
PUT YOURSELF
IN THE PICTURE

ARE THEY REALLY PRETTY AS A PICTURE? WALK INTO THE
WORLD'S MOST FAMOUS WORKS OF ART.

01 WILLY LOTT'S COTTAGE, SUFFOLK, ENGLAND

It's classic summertime England – a comely white cottage on the banks of a rippling river; golden meadows where haymakers toil; and billowing clouds, both white and grey-gloomy, suggestive of an impending shower. When John Constable completed *The Hay Wain* in 1821, it was not well received by the critics. But today it represents the romantic rural English idyll, now sadly long gone... Or gone-ish, anyway. You can actually still survey this quiet scene. The banks are overgrown and the water level higher (Suffolk is slowly sinking), but Willy Lott's house – named after its one-time tenant – still stands, an unlikely Arcadian icon to a gentler age.

Willy Lott's Cottage is not open to the general public, but nearby Bridge Cottage houses a Constable exhibition (see www.nationaltrust.org.uk).

02 MARQUESAS ISLANDS, FRENCH POLYNESIA

For Paul Gauguin, the coral-ringed specks of the South Pacific were an escape from the artifice of turn-of-the-century France. 'Here I enter Truth, become one with nature,' he wrote. And what nature it is.

The artist's Marquesas Islands are a land of fecund tropicality, of luminous colour, of beautiful, black-haired girls with flowers in their hair. Hiva Oa, a ludicrously lush isle of mountain peaks, gushing rivers and turquoise seas where Gauguin lived his last days, is no disappointment. To feel inspired by the great man's muse, visit the Maison du Jouir in Atuona, a replica of Gauguin's House of Pleasure, now home to works by local artists.

Visit French Polynesia from May to October, when the weather is drier and temperatures pleasantly cool.

03 VENICE, ITALY

Postcards for posh people – that was Canaletto's forte. When rich, 18th-century Englishmen thronged to Venice on their Grand Tours, many wanted reminders of its heady pleasures. Local boy Canaletto was a dab hand at *vedute* (detailed landscape) and pleased paying patrons with canvases of the Doges Palace, St Mark's Square, and the Grand Canal busy with garlanded gondolas (with any shabby bits diplomatically glossed over). Though a few *palazzi* may have crumbled since, the scenes remain remarkably unchanged; a punt along a

PATRICK FRILET » CORBIS

Venetian waterway today is to see the city of the past (just ignore the modern tourists).

Vaporetto water taxis are Venice's main public transport; buy tickets from booths at the stations. See www.hellovenezia.com.

○ GIVERNY, FRANCE

Life imitating art, or art come to life? Impressionist Claude Monet was as passionate about his garden as he was about painting it. He lived in a pretty pink stucco house in Giverny, 80km west of Paris, from 1883 to 1926, and in its grounds created his own inspirational subject matter: paths lined with rose bushes, avenues of cherry and apple trees, ponds draped with wisteria and those now-famous waterlilies. Open to the public since 1980, you can nose around the house and gardens, crossing his Japanese bridge and ducking beneath his weeping willows – literally a walk through Monet's masterpieces.

Visit in May or June when the rhododendrons and wisteria are in bloom (Monday, Wednesday and Friday are the quietest). See www.fondation-monet.fr.

○ MT FUJI, JAPAN

It's easy to put yourself in the picture when it's a *meisho-e* (a 'scene of a famous place'), although Katsushika Hokusai increased the challenge with the quantity and geographical spread of his work. The woodblock artist's *Thirty-six Views of Mount Fuji* (though they actually number 46) is a 19th-century series depicting the conical volcano as seen from various angles: reflected in Lake Kawaguchi, under Fukagawa's Mannen Bridge, from a teahouse at Koishikawa, and – most famously – enveloped by a monstrous wave off Kanagawa. It seems wherever you view Fuji from, the chances are Hokusai had it covered.

If travelling west by train from Tokyo, sit on the right-hand side for views of Fuji from around Shin-Fuji Station.

✪ GUERNICA, SPAIN

Thankfully the small town of Guernica looks nothing like Pablo Picasso's surrealist painting – that would be a frightening town indeed. But then, for three brief hours in April 1937, this Basque stronghold was a hellishly frightening place: 59 German and Italian planes bombed and strafed the place on its bustling market day; around 1650 lives were lost. Picasso conveyed this chaotic scene of distressed animals, screaming faces and prone bodies in his masterpiece, which resides in Madrid's Reina Sofía museum. In Guernica itself, now a thriving city, a ceramic-tile version of Picasso's work lines Calle Allende Salazar, lest people forget past horrors.

Guernica is 35km northeast of Bilbao; trains connect the two regularly, taking around 45 minutes.

✪ TLATELOLCO, MEXICO CITY, MEXICO

When it comes to painter Diego Rivera, it's impossible to separate the man, his masterpieces and his manor. Rivera's work is Mexican to the core: it depicts his homeland's historical battles, the

GLENN BEANLAND » LPI

oppression of its native cultures and its post-revolutionary struggles, often in gargantuan, propagandist proportions. His murals of Tlatelolco – an ancient city-in-a-lake, predating the Aztecs and once site of a market where 60,000 people at a time came to trade – provide a tantalising take on a site now in ruin. View the murals in the National Palace, then wander Tlatelolco's temple foundations and *tzompantli* (wall of skulls) and try to imagine what might have been.

The National Palace is open daily from 9am to 5pm; admission is free but ID is required.

✪ SKAGEN, DENMARK

Teetering on a sandy spit at the northernmost tip of Denmark, Skagen is the country's sunniest spot – and it's the quality of this abundant light that enticed artists to gather here. 'Are you a painter?' wrote Hans Christian Anderson after visiting in 1859. 'Then follow us up here' In the 1880s Peder Severin Krøyer did just that; his most famous work – *Summer Evening on Skagen's Southern Beach* – shows two ladies strolling away along the shore, their long dresses touched by a dusky glow. A century on, this quiet town's sands and skies have lost none of their magic.

Many of Krøyer's paintings, including Summer Evening, *are displayed in the Skagen Museum (www.skagensmuseum.dk).*

✪ ELDON, IOWA, USA

It was 1930 and the USA was staring down the Great Depression when artist Grant Wood was inspired to paint *American Gothic* as he drove around Eldon, Iowa. Two figures embody the persevering stoicism of rural middle America – a pinched-faced, pitchfork-wielding farmer and his prim-looking spinster daughter. They stand (looking suitably depressed) before a white clapboard house with an unusual Gothic window. The window so struck Wood that he was forced to stop and sketch it on the back of an envelope. The house is now a listed building, and visitors can borrow overalls and farms tools to recreate their own all-American moment outside.

Eldon is on Highway 16, 160km east of Des Moines. Admission to the American Gothic House Center is free. See www .wapellocounty.org.

✪ ARLES, FRANCE

Despite arriving on a bitter day in February 1888, Vincent Van Gogh found much inspiration in the Provençal town of Arles. He painted its Langlois Bridge, the surrounding wheat fields, its parks and its old ladies and one-eyed men – all with his signature swirling strokes and intense tones. But *Café Torrace at Night* is the painting you'll most want to step in to, with its bright, inviting veranda, a waiter serving tables, light dappling the cobbled street and an indigo sky a-sparkle with stars. The establishment is still there on Place du Forum, now called (no surprises) Café Van Gogh, so sit and raise a vino to Vincent.

Arles' Espace van Gogh, originally the hospital to which Van Gogh was admitted, is now a cultural centre (admission is free).

TOP SPOTS
TO GLAMP

AT THESE GLAMOROUS CAMPS ACROSS THE GLOBE,
YOU CAN GO WILD WITHOUT CRAMPING YOUR STYLE –
FIVE-STAR PERKS INCLUDED.

01 SAL SALIS NINGALOO REEF, AUSTRALIA

Soak up the 'wild bush luxury' of this high-end camp, a solar-powered retreat nestled in the white-sand dunes of Western Australia's Cape Range National Park. Nine spacious tents sit a stone's throw from Ningaloo, the world's greatest fringing coastal coral reef. Trimmings include linen-dressed beds and native herb soaps in en suite bathrooms. Outside, red kangaroos and wallaroos graze among the dunes as humpback whales breach offshore. Chow down on Mod Oz bush cuisine paired with orange sunsets over the Indian Ocean. Swim with whale sharks and manta rays, trek multicoloured gorges in search of black-footed rock wallabies or lie on the beach and gaze at the Milky Way.
During the wet season (16 January to 10 March, 2012), Sal Salis shuts down. See more at www.salsalis.com.au.

02 CLAYOQUOT WILDERNESS RESORT, CANADA

Adventures at Clayoquot, in a UNESCO-protected biosphere reserve on Vancouver Island, kick off with a bear orientation session, because you better behave correctly in bear country. Waterfront tents feature cedar-planked floors, Persian rugs and four-poster beds. Although most have en suite bathrooms, several come with private shower cabins just a short walk away (bear sightings possible). Spend time hiking or horse riding through old-growth rainforests, whale-watching and chowing down on locally caught wild salmon and meaty delights like bison burgers. Wind down with a soak in the wood-fired cedar hot tub and a body wrap with hand-harvested seaweed at the riverfront Healing Grounds spa.
Reachable by boat or floatplane only, Clayoquot is open from May to September. Plan your visit at www.wildretreat.com.

03 FOUR SEASONS TENTED CAMP GOLDEN TRIANGLE, THAILAND

Relive the adventures of 19th-century explorers at this uberluxe camp at the junction of Thailand, Laos and Myanmar (Burma). Dotting a hillside trail amid bamboo jungles, 15 free-standing tents come with elephant-tusk-styled doors, leather-and-hardwood bush chairs, hand-hammered copper bathtubs, outdoor decks and alfresco rain showers. Stays

BLOOMBERG »GETTY IMAGES

include every detail, from drinks and dining (jungle picnics, campfire barbecues and even formal meals) to encounters with local hill tribes, mahout training and elephant trekking – even spa pampering. Try the signature Mahout recovery treatment, during which camphor, lime and lemongrass poultices relax the body before a curative Asian massage.

Book the Hill Tribe Tent for most spectacular views of the Ruak River and the mountains of Laos (www.fourseasons .com/goldentriangle).

❂ SANCTUARY SWALA, TANZANIA

Spend a night under starry African skies at Sanctuary Swala, which takes luxury to the wildest level – quite literally. Towering acacia trees shade 12 tents in a private portion of northern Tanzania's Tarangire National Park, packed with elephant herds

and spectacular baobab trees. The camp may be in the midst of African bush, but there's no scrimping on style and perks, including a personal attendant. Open-plan tents are decked out with plush sofas, hand-sewn beaded fabrics and en suite bathrooms. Top off the Big Five sightings by spotting spiral-horned kudu and rapier-horned oryx. Post-game drive, sit around the campfire feasting on machalari stew and assorted Swahili treats.

Check out the luxury awaiting you at www.sanctuaryretreats.com.

❂ ECO RETREAT FINCA DE ARRIETA, SPAIN

Go all luxe on Lanzarote in Spain's Canary Islands. Year-round you can rule your very own yurt, from a cosy couple dwelling to a palatial family abode. The most lavish is Eco Yurt Royale, a Mongolian-style residence with a shaded day bed and bamboo dining gazebo on its own walled garden terrace. Inside there's plush fabrics, Balinese hardwood furniture, a skylight for stargazing and a marble-floored bathroom. Stroll down to a sandy beach or dip into the communal solar-heated swimming pool with sea and mountain views.

Lanzarote must-dos: jump off the pier at Arrieta beach, sip a chilled wine on the top of El Risco at sunset and visit Haria Saturday morning market.

✪ THREE CAMEL LODGE, MONGOLIA

The traditional tents of Mongolia's nomadic herders get seriously fancied up at Three Camel Lodge in the remote Gobi Desert. Its upmarket *gers* come with wood-burning stoves, hand-painted wood-framed beds and en suite bathrooms with felt slippers and camel milk lotions. Check out ancient petroglyphs, search for dinosaur fossils, spot black- and white-tailed gazelles, visit local families of herdspeople, ride through sand dunes atop a bactrian camel, or explore canyons and valleys of the Gobi-Altai Mountains on mountain bike or horseback. Savour *buuz* (Mongolian meat dumplings) at Bulagtai Restaurant, and down a shot of Mongolian vodka at the Thirsty Camel Bar.

The best times to visit are the shoulder seasons: May to June and September to October.

✪ AMAN-I-KHÁS, INDIA

Fancy yourself a Maharaja of bygone days at exclusive Aman-i-Khás, a wilderness camp on the edge of Rajasthan's Ranthambore National Park. Get lucky by spotting a tiger on the twice-daily safaris through desert terrain pockmarked with brushwood hills. Back at camp, the 10 tents echo the rich Moghul era. Fine cotton drapes separate the 'rooms', with plush trappings like oversized day beds and soaking tubs. And you'll love the lawn dinners of fine Indian cuisine, with chutneys, poppadoms and naan served outside, as the chef whips up tandoor treats. Unwind with a Choorna Sweda poultice treatment in the spa tent, using Ayurvedic herbs from the camp's organic garden.

The camp is set up annually from October until the end of April, the best period for wildlife spotting.

✪ CHOBE UNDER CANVAS, BOTSWANA

Get up close and personal with Botswana's wildlife at this mobile camp inside the game-rich Chobe National Park. Accommodating just 10 guests at a time, its tents come with spacious beds, crisp linens, en suite bathrooms and shady verandas. Spend your days scouting herds of buffalo or the elusive oribi antelope. Glide among hundreds of elephant cavorting in the cooling waters on a river cruise, as herds of sable wander the water's edge. Then swap safari stories over cocktails around a blazing fire and dine on bush treats beneath star-speckled African skies. Don't forget to bring earplugs to keep out the noise of roaring lions.

Your hosts, &Beyond, operate 12 lodges across southern Africa. See www.and beyondafrica.com.

JEFFREY L ROTMAN >>CORBIS

✪ THE RESORT AT PAWS UP, USA

Indulge your cowboy/girl fantasies as you wander the 37,000 acres of western wilderness surrounding this rural-glam hideaway in Montana. Glampers stay in one of four lavish camps with fancy canvas homes, and the chef creates gourmet fare with local ingredients – handmade elk sausages or juicy pancakes with freshly picked huckleberries, anyone? Bond around a bonfire as your butler attends to whims like s'mores with dark chocolate. Burn off all the fine food by rappelling off a cliff or horse riding through conifer forests. Perk up with pre-breakfast yoga among the ponderosa pine and wrap up with a hot-stone massage at the tented Spa Town.
The camps are open from late May to October. For the best rates, go before mid-June or after 4 September.

✪ PATAGONIA CAMP, CHILE

Wilderness is paired with eco-chic charms at Patagonia Camp on the edge of Torres del Paine National Park. Flecking the dense beech forests of Lake Toro, 18 plush yurts offer dramatic vistas of the Paine Massif from private terraces. Inside the heated domes, locally woven fabrics and handcrafted furniture make up the pretty decor. Creature comforts include en suite bathrooms and king-sized beds. Pair your active pursuits – lots and lots of hikes included – with culinary pleasures back at camp, where the chef prepares slow-roasted Magellanic lamb while you imbibe pisco sours and fine Chilean wines.
Patagonia Camp (open from early September to late April) is best to visit during spring and autumn, when the colours are more vibrant and the crowds fewer.

SLURPING SOUP
ACROSS
THE GLOBE

A WARMING STAPLE THE WORLD OVER –
BUT WHO KNEW THERE WERE SO MANY FINE FLAVOURS?

01 PHO, HANOI, VIETNAM

Beef noodle soup for breakfast? Once you've tasted a good *pho,* you'll crave it for lunch and dinner, too. *Pho* is the more-ish national dish of Vietnam, though its genesis is relatively recent. In the early 20th century the colonising French introduced beef stock to local cooks, who threw in some chillies, fish sauce, spices and rice noodles to give it a local twist. The dish originates from the country's north and, though now widespread, Hanoi is still the *pho*cal point. Every morning, street-side stands and no-frills restaurants go into beef-slicing, broth-boiling overdrive, producing bowl after bowl of Asian ambrosia for the passing crowds.

Vietnam's rainy season runs from May to September; visit from November to April for drier, cooler weather.

02 AJIACO, BOGOTÁ, COLOMBIA

Soup is traditionally a starter, right? But begin your dinner with a bowl of *ajiaco santafereño* and you won't be eating again for a while. This dense Colombian super-fuel food combines three different types of potato – yellow *papas criollas* for thickening, plus waxy red *sabaneras* and squishier white *pastusa* – infused with handfuls of *gausca,* an aromatic herb. And that's just how the native Chibcha people left it. Subsequently the Spanish rocked up, liked what they tasted but added some protein (chicken) and a side of cream to concoct the belly-warmer now beloved across Bogotá and beyond.

In Bogotá try the Sopas de Mamá y Postres de la Abuela (Soups of Mum and Grandmother's Desserts) restaurant chain.

03 LOCRO DE PAPAS, ANDEAN HIGHLANDS, ECUADOR

You need something to warm your cockles in the Ecuadorian Andes: villages teeter at breath-stealing altitudes, and nights can be cold indeed. Given this land is the home of the potato, it's no surprise the traditional hot belly-filler in these parts is hearty *locro de papas* – potato soup. The Spanish conquistadores first came across it in the 1560s, and its popularity hasn't waned since. Variants exist (there's always garlic and hot peppers, often cheese and avocado, and sometimes beef or guinea pig), but after a day hiking up volcanoes or across

parámo, a generous dollop of any kind is more than welcome.

Cotopaxi National Park, a 1½-hour drive south of capital Quito, offers a range of trekking and horse-riding trails.

✪ BORSCHT, UKRAINE

The first rule of botany states that the country with the most variants of a particular species is probably where that species originated. Translate this to cuisine and Ukraine is the top contender for the homeland of *borscht*. Although the eye-poppingly purple beetroot soup is slurped across Eastern Europe – filling tummies in Poland, Russia, Lithuania and beyond – it's in Ukraine that you'll find the greatest glut of recipes, which differ from Kiev to Lviv to Odessa. It always looks utterly fabulous, though the girlie colouring is offset by a manly accompaniment of *pampushky* (fried doughnuts), which turn this shrinking violet into a real meal.

Trains are the best way of getting around Ukraine; a few words of Russian will help when booking tickets.

✪ OBE ATA, NIGERIA

Locals call it a pick-me-up, a medicinal dish to reinvigorate those feeling under the weather. The uninitiated might call it hell-in-a-ladle. It doesn't necessarily taste bad; it's just like eating Satan's pitchfork, fresh from the furnace. Essentially Nigeria's national dish, *obe ata* (pepper soup) is a fiery beast, especially if Scotch bonnet chillies are in the mix. It can also have some unusual ingredients, including tripe, dried fish and the whole head of

GREG ELMS » LPI

a goat. But if you can brave a bowl on the streets of Lagos, know that you're experiencing the real taste of West Africa. *Temperatures in Nigeria are hot year-round, though October to January is a little cooler. Check security advice before travelling.*

✪ WATERZOOI, GHENT, BELGIUM

There's something fishy going on in Ghent. Inventor of the Flemish seafood-soup, *waterzooi,* this river-port city now seems to be using chicken in the dish... This preference for poultry allegedly occurred when Ghent's waterways became polluted, killing off the recipe's main ingredient. Thankfully, today you can still find the original fish version (often made with pike, carp or bass) in the narrow medieval streets of the Patershol quarter. Here restaurants cook up the soup with various vegies and thicken it with egg yolks and cream. Hunks of bread are provided for dunking, and a Belgian beer is near-obligatory for washing it down.

Ghent is 30 minutes by train from Brussels. Visit in July for the Gentse Feesten music and theatre festival.

✪ CULLEN SKINK, MORAYSHIRE, SCOTLAND

If you saw it on a menu, you'd just have to try it, wouldn't you? First cooked up on Scotland's northeast coast, in the comely village of Cullen, this irresistibly named soup used to sustain the sailors of the Moray Firth – back when fish were both abundant and a fair bit cheaper than the traditional beef base. Its ingredients are simple yet simply superb: the finest locally smoked Finnan haddock, the best Buchan tatties, plus onions and cream. And though the dish has spread beyond Cullen's harbour, for a taste of skink at its most authentic, try it at the 18th-century Seafield Hotel.

Cullen is a 2½-hour bus ride from Aberdeen. The Seafield is at 17–19 Seafield St (www.theseafieldarms.co.uk).

✪ CALLALOO, TRINIDAD

Trinidad itself is a bit of a soup. Here, African, Indian, Spanish, French, Chinese and Native American influences are stirred together, and simmered under the hot Caribbean sun to make a tasty, addictive treat of an island, best washed down with a slug of Black Label rum. But one dish prevails out of this cultural cook-up: *callaloo.* A rich green gloop made from fresh dasheen leaves and pureed okra, perhaps with coconut and delicious with chunks of crab, its flavours are as zingy as a Trinidadian street party. Hunt out a simple eatery, order *callaloo* and *foo-foo* (pounded plantains), and melt into the mix.

Trinidad's Carnival, the region's biggest, will take place on 20–21 February.

✪ CLAM CHOWDER, NEW ENGLAND, USA

In the kitchens of New England, clam chowder (or *chowda,* in Bostonian) is a very serious business. So serious, in fact, that a law was almost passed in the 1930s to ban tomatoes from its mollusc mix. You see, tomatoes mean Manhattan chowder – a newfangled New Yorker fad and literally a different kettle of fish. Threaten this seafood soup with fruit in New England and you might as well declare your support for the Yankees. No, from Massachusetts to Maine, chowder is made with cream. Period. Very good it can be, too. And if it's not, just don't ask for ketchup...

Try a range of soup varieties at Rhode Island's Newport Chowder Cook-Off, held every June.

✪ GAZPACHO, ANDALUCÍA, SPAIN

It's a poor man's supper – but it tastes so good. For the hard-up labourers toiling in the fields, *gazpacho* was a way to make something of almost nothing: a stale crust of bread softened by garlic, vinegar and a slosh of olive oil. But from its humble roots, *gazpacho* (perhaps drawn from the Arabic 'caspa', meaning fragments) has become a dish of kings. During the stultifying Andalucían summer, when the tomatoes and peppers are at their very ripest, and when all you can face eating is something refreshing and cool, *gazpacho* is just the dish to tantalise torpid tastebuds.

In July and August, temperatures in Andalucía soar over 40°C. April to June is best for mild weather and lush countryside.

JESÚS OCHOA » LP

YOU WON'T BE EATING AGAIN FOR A WHILE IF YOU BEGIN YOUR MEAL WITH AJIACO IN COLOMBIA

WAYS TO BE A WORLD CHAMPION

EVEN IF YOU'RE NOT COMPETING IN THE LONDON OLYMPICS, DON'T LET A LACK OF TALENT KEEP YOU FROM TAKING A STAB AT LIFTING A WINNER'S TROPHY.

01 WIFE-CARRYING, FINLAND

The world championship of wife-carrying turns 20 this year; a good occasion to partake in Eukonkannon MM-kisat, Finland's (strictly) 253.5m obstacle course of sand, gravel and grass held annually in July in Sonkajärvi. This proud Finnish tradition involves a man negotiating the course while carrying his wife (or a friend's or neighbour's in a pinch), usually upside-down, with her legs wrapped around the man's neck. It's €50 (US$71.50) to participate, or the same to protest a winner, and is governed by the decree that 'everyone must have fun'. If you doubt the need for the existence of this rising sport, consider the organisation's own description: 'Wife-carrying is an attitude towards life.' And it's a winning attitude at that.

For information on how to participate, see www.eukonkanto.fi.

02 WORLD BEARD & MOUSTACHE CHAMPIONSHIP, USA

On to the biggest event of all. If hair grows on your face, pick a category in this globe-trotting event (it was in Norway in 2011 and is scheduled to be in the USA in 2012) and start cultivating your whiskers in time for this May contest. Created in Germany in 1990, contestants frequently put as much effort into their outfits (Edwardian suits etc) as the hairy creations on their faces. But, oh, those bushy Hungarian, Garibaldi, musketeer and Dali and Fu Manchu moustaches! The 'partial beard' categories are particular favourites, but none beats the unpredictability and wonder of a conceptualised freestyle moustache. Sorry London, your Olympics is too clean-cut for some of us.

The 2012 competition is expected to be held in San Francisco or Washington, DC. For updates see www.worldbeard championships.com.

03 ROCK PAPER SCISSORS, CANADA

The immortal game of rock/paper/scissors – officially formalised by the World RPS Society in London in 1848 – takes the international stage each year in Canada, where competitors throw down one of the three in hope of taking away a C$10,000 (US$9400) prize. And, of course, the title of RPS champ. Believe it or not, there's actually a bit of science to it. Beginners are more prone to 'double down' (take the same option twice in a row) and tend to see the 'rock' as strongest. The advice is to keep it loose, keep it random and think 'paper' when in doubt. Usually staged in Toronto, this year the RPS World Society is expecting to convene in late summer in Banff.

For tips on not looking like a beginner, and updates on dates, see www .worldrps.com.

✪ WORLD STONE SKIMMING CHAMPIONSHIP, EASEDALE ISLAND, SCOTLAND

Requiring only slightly more talent than rock/paper/scissors, this Scottish tradition asks you to stand at the shorelines of an old slate-mining island, pick a stone out of a provided yellow bucket and slide it across the surface – if it skips at least three times, you're eligible...to be champion of the world. Note that it's distance travelled rather than the number of skips that takes the prize in this event. Held on the last Sunday in September, the champ wins a cup – but bring a team for the chance to win the incomparably named Puffer Trophy.

Ferries to the island cost £1.50 (US$2.50) and leave from Ellenabeich, about 25km south of Oban on the west coast. For more on the island see www.easdale.org.

✪ BEST BAGGERS CONTEST, USA

When they're good, they're good – and we watch mesmerised. Grocery bagging is a serious business; the best baggers can scientifically fill every cubic inch with bread, milk and eggs, and then work

DAVID WHITE »ALAMY

WIFE-CARRYING IS AN ATTITUDE TOWARDS LIFE, THEY SAY IN FINLAND

deli meats and instant sauces into the crevices. Now it's your turn. Every year, USA regional competitions culminate with a national Best Baggers Contest, hosted by the National Grocers Association. Plan ahead and practise your bagging. If you properly distribute the weight and complete your bagging with lightning speed while maintaining a friendly attitude, you can be the champ. Held in mid-February, it turns 25 in 2012.

The first competition pitted the best Texan and Oklahoman grocers against each other. Now it's global. See www.national grocers.com for details.

✪ AIR GUITAR, OULU, FINLAND

What's up with Finland? Beyond wife-carrying (and mobile-phone throwing) contests, there's this king of self-made inspiration: air guitar. Oulu's Music Video Festival is a real-deal four-day event held in late August, and has upped the ante in the past 15 years with its annual contest, which has prompted 'air sex' spin-offs in some corners of the globe – don't ask. Regional contests blanket the globe, but Oulu's brings out the dirtiest power chords and quickest finger-taps.

Sited on the Bay of Bothnia, Oulu is one of Finland's most scenic cities. See www .airguitarworldchampionships.com for more on the town's signature competition.

✪ GURNING, ENGLAND

Ever not liked what you see in the mirror? Well perhaps gurning is for you. The practice of contorting your face into hideous expressions – best achieved if you start off ugly and toothless – is linked with the Egremeont Crab Festival, which has been held in this Cumbrian town in northern England since 1267. The World Gurning Championships feature all sorts of grins, grimaces, frowns and scowls, all posed while wearing a horse collar. But beware: contestants take it very seriously. One of the all-time greats, Peter Jackman, actually had his teeth removed to be a better gurner. It worked, too.

Get gurning-friendly lodging tips at www .egremontcrabfair.com.

✪ NOODLING, OKLAHOMA, USA

Slog through sandy banks in muddy creeks and rivers, stick your hands blindly into slimy holes that could house a gator or beaver, and hope, hope, hope that a 22kg bottom-feeder catfish (a truly hideous breed) snaps onto your arm so you can hoist it out. That's noodling for you – and since 2001 the place to compete has been Paul's Valley in Oklahoma (about 96km south of Oklahoma City), which hosts a full-on competition each year in late June or early July. The tradition is linked to Native Americans, who fished using this method, though their injury rates are unknown.

To get inspired, see Oklahoma film-maker Bradley Beesley's unforgettable documen-tary, and get entry details and info on the 2012 event, at www.okienoodling.com.

✪ SNOW FIGHT! HOKKAIDO, JAPAN

Boredom and blizzards are mixed (at last!) in Hokkaido to create a seriously upgraded version of the ol' winter pastime of snowball fights. The Showa-Shinzan International Yukigassen

(Japanese for 'snow fight') is an icy take on 'capture the flag', with teams of seven players, 90 snowballs and one mission: to capture the opponents' flag or tally points through body hits. Held since 1988 each February, the competition is open to all – but applications should be made early (they open in December), as 2500 teams sign up quickly. The notion of *yukigassen* has spread, with regional championships around the word, from Norway to Saskatchewan. But this is still the biggest of the snow rumbles.

Showa-Shinzan is a mountain formed only in 1943, following a series of earthquakes. You can get here by train or bus from Sapporo in under two hours.

✪ ARGUNGU INTERNATIONAL FISH FESTIVAL, NIGERIA

Here's another hand-fishing classic. You have four crazy hours, and at least 7000 fellows at your side, to find the biggest fish in the Malan Fada River – with your hands. No fishing lines for miles. On the shore, you'll see robed revellers banging drums and cheering you on, as you wade chin deep in the muddy water. Press on, the champ gets one million Nigerian Naira (about US$6400) and – you'll love this – a tricycle. It's been a festival devoted to peace in the region since 1934, usually held in March.

The best accommodation is 100km away in the town of Sokoto.

ERSOY EMIN » ALAMY

MIND THAT DOORWAY – THE WORLD BEARD & MOUSTACHE CHAMPIONSHIPS ARE HELD IN CARSON CITY, NEVADA

UK OUTSIDE THE
OLYMPICS

AWAY FROM SPRINTING, SWIMMING AND SOMERSAULTS,
ONE OF THE WORLD'S GOLD-MEDAL DESTINATIONS AWAITS

01 TACKLE A TRAIL

England and Wales' National Trails, and Scotland's Long Distance Routes, offer gentler activity than the synchronised swimming or Greco-Roman wrestling on offer in London. This year is the 40th anniversary of the creation of the National Trail following the Ridgeway: an ancient trackway that's been in use by Britons for at least 5000 years. It begins close to the stone circle of Avebury in Wiltshire and winds over rolling chalk downland, giving way to narrow forest paths before finishing at the wonderful viewpoint of Ivinghoe Beacon in the Chiltern Hills.

This 140km path can be done in a week or as a series of shorter walks, with good B&Bs close by. See www.nationaltrails.co.uk.

02 FOOTBALL

When the Olympics aren't on it is football (soccer) that hogs the headlines. Anywhere in the country, with the arguable exception of the rugby-mad southwest, you'll find a professional game kicking off at 3pm on a Saturday. English Premier League (EPL) tickets can be hard to get, especially for big teams, but visiting often well-supported lower-league clubs can be lots of fun, easier to arrange and much cheaper. London alone has nine professional sides outside the top flight. Wales' big boys scrap it out with English clubs, while Scotland goes it alone. A crisp afternoon visit to Stirling Albion, Inverness Caledonian Thistle or Brechin City will be a marvellous, undiluted taste of British sporting life.

Football fans will just love the Scottish Football Museum (www.scottish footballmuseum.org.uk), at Hampden Park, Glasgow, which is crammed full of impressive memorabilia.

03 BELFAST'S BIG SHIP

Northern Ireland's still underrated capital makes much of its *Titanic* associations (see p196). That most famous of sinking ships was built in the city's Harland & Wolff shipyards and set sail from Southampton a hundred years ago this year. Belfast offers walking and boat tours as well as exhibitions celebrating the ship and the city's association with it, and activity will reach a crescendo in 2012. Though this is one story with a most unhappy ending, locals will tell you 'she was all right when she left here'.

The Titanic Belfast Visitor Attraction is an exhibition centre due to open in 2012, at

PHOTONTRAPPIST »ALAMY

the head of the slipways in the heart of the Titanic Quarter.

✪ NORTHUMBERLAND

One of Britain's most remote corners has also been one of its most eagerly fought over. Today's Northumberland was the battleground between squabbling English and Scots for centuries. The marks of history are all over this rugged, dramatic landscape, from wonderful castles at Bamburgh (best viewed while swimming off the superb beach below) and Alnwick to Lindisfarne Priory on Holy Island and, of course, Hadrian's Wall, now the setting for walking and cycling routes. Much of the county is within Northumberland National Park, which is blissfully quiet compared with others in the UK.

The boisterous city of Newcastle-upon-Tyne is a great start or finish point for a few days here.

✪ THE SIZZLING SOUTH COAST

The south coast of England has much more to offer visitors than the popular day trip from London to Brighton. In autumn this year, Portsmouth's Historic Dockyard will open the new Mary Rose Museum, with better views than ever before of the remains of Henry VIII's warship. Across the Solent, Southampton's maritime connections will be celebrated in July when P&O celebrates 175 years of operation by welcoming seven of its ships to the city's waters. From either city you can take a ferry or even (pay attention, retro transport buffs) a hovercraft to the Isle of Wight. Tube trains from 1938 (more historical transport) now chug along between Ryde Pier Head and Shanklin.

Check out other things to see and do on the coast at www.visitsoutheastengland.com.

✪ A BEATLE'S BRITAIN

A Paul McCartney road trip round Britain will take you to some wonderful corners of the country – the perfect iPod accompaniment being the timeless Wings stomper *Live and Let Die,* recorded 40 years ago this November. Macca's childhood home at 20 Forthlin Road, Liverpool can be visited on a National Trust tour that also visits Mendips, where John Lennon spent his formative years. The Beatles sights of Merseyside are well known, but less obvious is a journey to Scotland's Mull of Kintyre, the inspiration for Wings' 1977 hit single, and where McCartney still maintains a Highland retreat. Here you can do some back-to-nature hiking and sample superb locally caught seafood.

Time your visit to the Mull of Kintyre for the traditional Scottish music festival (www.mokfest.com), held in Campbeltown in late August.

✪ COTSWOLDS OLYMPICKS

Did you know Britain hosts an Olympic Games every year? Since 1612, Dover's Hill near Chipping Campden in Gloucestershire

IAN HORROCKS/NEWCASTLE UNITED » GETTY IMAGES

DANNY SIMPSON (R) OF NEWCASTLE CHALLENGES JAVIER HERNANDEZ OF MANCHESTER UNITED IN NEWCASTLE UPON TYNE, APRIL 2011

has intermittently hosted the Cotswolds Olympicks. The hill shares its name with Robert Dover, a local lawyer who created the games with the approval of King James I. Events in the modern version include some familiar standards like cross-country running, but it is the more eccentric pursuits like piano smashing, shin kicking and dwile flonking – where competitors attempt to slap encircling competitors with beer-sodden rags and drinking penalties result in mass drunkenness – draw the big crowds.

For the 400th anniversary in 2012, a week of cultural events is planned as well as the games themselves, which take place on 1 June (see www.olimpickgames.co.uk).

✪ OUTDOOR SWIMMING

Over the past few years, the Outdoor Swimming Society and like-minded individuals have promoted the delights of exploring the rivers, lakes and seas around the UK. Provided you're not expecting tropical temperatures, you could consider doing the same. Swimming the River Cam at Grantchester Meadows is a time-honoured delight, as is cooling off in a Lake District tarn on a summer's day. Perhaps the best way to start is by exploring some of the seaside lidos of Devon and Cornwall – Plymouth and Penzance both have wonderful, enormous art deco lidos. Even if you jump in and jump straight out again, you'll have a mad grin on your face all day.

Check out the Outdoor Swimming Society's site (www.oss.org.uk) and bring warm clothes, even in high summer.

✪ BRITISH SEASIDE

Largs in Scotland is a classic slice of British seaside. It's one of Scotland's best spots on a sunny day, with grassy banks running down into the Firth of Clyde. And down on the Esplanade you'll find Nardini's. Hailed by many as the best ice-cream parlour in Britain, it is housed in an art deco delight of a building and offers 32 flavours of gelato. If you can move after that, Vikingar! (Largs' other main draw) tells the story of the Vikings in Scotland.

Largs is an easy day trip from Glasgow, itself an essential stop on any tour of underrated Britain.

✪ WALES' THOROUGHLY MODERN OLD-SCHOOL RAILWAYS

Wales' little trains have stolen many hearts. The network, mostly made up of old industrial lines lovingly preserved by volunteer enthusiasts, will be at its greatest-ever extent in 2012. The completion of the Welsh Highland Railway means that not only can you take the dramatic journey through Snowdonia from Caernarfon to Porthmadog, but once there you also have a choice of two additional services: the Welsh Highland Heritage Line and the longer Ffestiniog Railway, which travels along another scenic stretch. You can connect to mainline services at Porthmadog, but it's a good bet you won't want to leave these charming train lines and the inspirational people who run them.

A discount card offering 20% off trips and deals on local accommodation is available at www.greatlittletrainsofwales.co.uk.

THE GREATEST
GUILTY
PLEASURES

EVERYONE NEEDS TO INDULGE THEIR VICES EVERY NOW AND THEN

01 LET THE GOOD TIMES ROLL, LAS VEGAS, NEVADA, USA

Sin City – the setting for iconic tales of modern excess, from Hunter Thompson's *Fear and Loathing in Las Vegas* to the film *The Hangover,* Vegas has become synonymous with overindulgence and cutting loose. It boasts more gambling casinos than any other city on the planet, plus the world's largest food buffet and largest strip club, along with 15 of the world's 20 largest hotels. There are no statistics for annual alcohol consumption in Vegas, but presumably it would boggle the mind. In a city that promotes itself with the slogan, 'What happens in Vegas, stays in Vegas', anything can happen – and usually does.

Somewhat surprisingly, Las Vegas is also kid-friendly. Check out www.vegaskids .info for G- and PG-rated fun.

02 SMOKE LIKE AN EGYPTIAN, CAIRO, EGYPT

There's something alluring about the *shisha* – the ubiquitous waterpipe smoked by Egyptian men. Maybe it's the bubbling of the water in the glass base, maybe it's the curly hose you draw on, or maybe it's the ornate architecture of the brass stem capped with a clay bowl. Trying one at a coffee shop is an essential way to get a taste of Egyptian culture. Order a *hagar* (Arabic for 'stone') of sticky tobacco (many tourists like apple flavour, while locals prefer plain), and enjoy with tea, coffee or *karkadai* (brewed from hibiscus leaves).

Cairo's most famous coffeehouse is Fishawi's, at Khan al-Khalili market.

03 EAT DURING RAMADAN, VAN, TURKEY

Non-Muslims who are visiting Muslim countries during Ramadan are not expected to obey the fast. But finding somewhere discreet to eat, or even enjoy a cup of tea, can sometimes be a challenge. Restaurants and coffee shops all appear closed, but in some places, like Van in eastern Turkey (where the holiday is called Ramazan), look for shops with windows covered with newspaper. The chances are that inside you'll find a cafe where men are secretly drinking tea, smoking cigarettes and eating snacks; it's something like a Ramadan speakeasy. You'll be welcomed in (women, too). Just

RICHARD CUMMINS » LPI

don't dilly-dally – walk right in and close the door quickly behind you!

To learn more about Ramazan in Turkey, see www.turkeytravelplanner.com /Religion/ramazan.

✪ LET LOOSE AT A BEACH PARTY, KO PHA-NGAN, THAILAND

Few places on the planet are as perfect for shedding your inhibitions as Ko Pha-Ngan, especially during the epic Full Moon parties, which claim to be the biggest beach bashes in the world. With cheap Thai whiskey – and plenty of other mind-altering substances – flowing freely, barely clad bodies dancing on the sand, loud music, bonfires and a vibe of unadulterated hedonism, there's no reason to resist getting swept up in it all. Maybe best of all, you can sleep it off the next day, lazing on gorgeous beaches and swimming in the clear emerald sea – a sure-fire hangover cure.

Near the party beach of Hat Rin, Phangan Buri Resort and Spa is an Lonely Planet author–recommended hotel. See www .phangan buriresort.com.

✪ SLEEP LIKE ROYALTY, JAIPUR, INDIA

Jaipur's first palace, built back in 1727, is now one of the world's top heritage hotels. It's an exquisite example of Mughal archi-tecture, with fluted archways, gold-leafed ceilings, marble bathrooms, ivory furniture and crystal chandeliers: impeccably classy and inarguably authentic. Guests are made to feel like royalty. If you're up for a splurge, go for the Shahi Mahal Presidential Suite, which costs US$40,000 per night (yes, that's 40,000 and no, it's not rupees) and comes with a private pool, personal spa and dedicated servants (in case you've accidentally left yours at home).

Each March Jaipur hosts the Elephant Festival, when painted pachyderms pa-rade through the streets before competing in races, polo matches and tugs-of-war against teams of men.

✪ CLOG YOUR ARTERIES, CHANDLER, ARIZONA, USA

With specialities like the 'Quadruple Bypass Burger' (said to weigh in at 8000 calories), 'Flatliner Fries' (deep-fried in pure lard) and the 'Butterfat Shake', the Heart Attack Grill stands wholeheartedly behind its motto: 'Taste worth dying for!' Waitresses dressed up like nurses take orders on a prescription pad and will take you out to your car in a wheelchair if you manage to finish a Quadruple Bypass. You can buy beer and smokes (there are candy cigarettes for the kids), but no diet soda. It's so obscenely unhealthy, that even the restaurant's owner calls the food 'nutritional pornography'.

Drop in to 6185 W Chandler Blvd, Chandler. It's open 11am to 8.30pm Monday to Saturday, and 11am to 3pm Sunday.

✪ BURN SOME RUBBER, FLORENCE, ITALY

Florence is one of the art capitals of the world, blessed with an abundance of palaces, churches and museums that are loaded with best-in-show examples of Renaissance painting, sculpture and architecture. But if you get bored with that trove of artistic perfection (or the horrendous queues, don't allow yourself to feel like an uncultured dolt. Instead, experience a different form of legendary Italian design – rent a Ferrari. Half-day tours of the Tuscany countryside put you behind the wheel and allow you to drive along the famed Mille Miglia road race route and through the gorgeous Chianti hills, past vineyards and villages. Tour leaders teach you how to handle these earthbound rockets and keep you from getting lost.

Prices for a half-day tour start at €850 (US$1215). See more at www.red-travel.com.

✪ TASTE DESSERT HEAVEN, BANGKOK, THAILAND

Order up a piece of Madagascar chocolate cake, a dab of strawberry-chocolate mousse, a spoonful of champagne sherbet and some crème brûlée topped with shaved truffles, then serve them together on a plate with edible gold leaf. Add a glass of the rare Moyet Tres Vieille Grande No 7, and you've just been served the Chocolate Variation, one of the most expensive desserts in the world. It's created at Mezzaluna in Bangkok, where the dining room hovers 65 storeys over the city and offers breathtaking views. You may truly gasp, however, when you get the bill – US$640 for the dessert alone!

For cheaper Thai delicacies in Bangkok, head for the stalls at Talad Loong Perm market.

✪ DRINK LIKE A NOMAD, MONGOLIA

Visit a felt tent (called a *ger*) on the Mongolian steppes, and you'll likely find yourself handed a large bowl of *airag* – Mongolian moonshine made from fermented horse milk. This concoction is a bit sour, and sometimes carries quite a kick, but drunkenness will *always* follow – less from the potency than from the sheer quantity you'll be expected to imbibe. And if the Genghis Khan–brand vodka comes out, then you'd better brace yourself. It will have to be finished off as well, because the bottle tops are not resealable. Don't be too surprised if, by the end of the night, you hear someone being noisily sick outside. *The best airag is said to come from Dundgov or Middle Gobi province, south of Mongolia's capital Ulan Bataar.*

✪ SAMPLE A SPLIFF IN THE RED LIGHT DISTRICT, AMSTERDAM, NETHERLANDS

Famous as the world's capital of legalised vice, Amsterdam's De Wallen district is dotted with comfy 'coffeeshops' where (unless the proposed tourist ban goes ahead) you can order up grams of marijuana loose or pre-rolled into joints. There are many other establishments featuring lingerie-clad women in the red-lit windows that give the area its nickname; even if you're not interested in sampling their services, a stop at the Prostitution Information Centre is fascinating. You can ask questions about anything and join a tour of a working brothel.

For more about the Prostitution Information Centre, visit www.pic-amsterdam.com.

ARIADNE VAN ZANDBERGEN » LPI

NOW THAT'S A SERIOUS SMOKE BREAK – ROSETTA, EGYPT

BEST PLACES TO
TRUNDLE IN A TRAM

TURN A BASIC JOURNEY INTO A THING OF BEAUTY BY HOPPING ON ONE OF THE WORLD'S MOST SUPER STREETCARS.

01 SAN FRANCISCO, USA

Commuting is just better in San Francisco. Here, every morning can be injected with a little movie magic. So familiar from supporting roles on the silver screen, the city's antique cablecars are more theme park than public transport: passengers dangle off the sides as the tring-tringing trolleys whizz down (or wheeze up) the perilously perpendicular roads, blasted by salty sea breeze. Or try the streetcars instead: the F Line is similarly retro, employing a glamorous fleet of heritage carriages to connect the rainbow-flag-flying Castro district to the downtown skyscrapers and bustling Waterfront beyond, all in flamboyant San Fran style.

One-/three-/seven-day Passports, valid for all public transport in the city, cost $13/20/26. See www.sfmta.com.

02 ISTANBUL, TURKEY

It's slow. It's small. And it's always tinkling its bell to clear the tracks ahead of ambling İstanbulites. But these minor inconveniences simply make the old tram that trundles up and down İstiklal Caddesi all the more endearing. The rattly cars first started linking the Beyoglu district's Tünel Station with Taksim Square in the 19th century. Long out of service, the compact streetcars were reinstated in the 1990s, to convey the weary and unhurried along freshly pedestrianised and gentrified Istikal: a piece of history traversing the avenue of shops and buzzy cafes that's now the hip hub of European İstanbul.

Jetons (tokens) must be bought before boarding the tram; they're available from machines and some newspaper kiosks.

03 FLANDERS, BELGIUM

There's something satisfyingly complete – as well as scenically refreshing – about Belgium's Coast Tram. The Kusttram hugs the country's entire North Sea shore, tracing the 68km Flanders shoreline from De Panne (near the French border) to Knokke-Heist (near the Dutch) – a traverse of a nation in just two hours, with sand dune and sea views all the way. There's more, too: Surrealism started hereabouts, and many suitably strange sculptures pass by the tram window. Less odd are the beachside

MITCHELL FUNK » GETTY IMAGES

cafes: stop off at charming De Haan to eat *moules frites* in sight of the sea.

A Coast Tram day pass costs €5 (US$7); trams leave every 20/30 minutes in summer/winter.

✪ MELBOURNE, AUSTRALIA

There's a ton of tram tracks in Melbourne; the Australian city is home to the largest network in the world. But in this streetcar spaghetti, one line stands out. Not only does 96 tram shuttle more passengers than any other, but it is also the *coolest*. Starting amid the boho boutiques and edgy art galleries of Fitzroy, there's time to shop for rare vinyl and organic espresso before hopping aboard for the 50-minute trundle – via the Central Business District and Albert Park – to cosmopolitan St Kilda, for over-spilling cafes, the cheery cheese of Luna Park and the city's finest beach.

Mart 130 at Middle Park tram stop serves fine breakfasts and brunches in the converted station master's house.

✪ BUDAPEST, HUNGARY

The trams that waddle around the Hungarian capital are real streetcar survivors. Budapest was one of the first cities in the world to embrace electric trams, with its first line opening in 1887. Two World Wars and decades of Communism saw the network damaged and depleted, and today it's a shadow of its former self. But it endures – and

the distinctive yellow carriages are still the best way to travel. For a cheap and atmospheric tour, hop on Line 2 for close-ups of the grand Parliament and views to Buda Castle opposite, as the tram follows the blue(ish) sweep of the Danube.

Line 2 travels along the Pest side of the river, from Jaszai Mari Ter to Vagohid. See www.bkv.hu.

✪ LISBON, PORTUGAL

A series of seven hills make a pretty perch for the Portuguese capital – and a lung-testing prospect for anyone walking in it. Luckily Lisbon has a glorious solution: its tram network is extensive, cheap as a trademark custard tart and effortlessly atmospheric, still utilising vintage, wood-panelled streetcars to squeeze down the narrow alleyways. Line 28 is best: rattle from the lofty eyrie of white-domed Basilica da Estrela, skimming the higgle-piggle of Barrio Alto and the rooftops of Alfama (serenaded by the melancholy melodies of *fado*), to reach Graca, the place where locals go to watch the sun set on their scenic city.

Line 28 takes around 45 minutes to ride from start to finish. Single tickets can be purchased from the driver.

✪ AMSTERDAM, NETHERLANDS

Purists may feel bikes are the best way to access Amsterdam's nooks and crannies. That's fine in the sunshine, but for all those damper Dutch days, the tram rules this slender-streeted city. Centraal Station is the obvious start-point – from this domineering Neo-Renaissance terminus, myriad lines wriggle outwards. The most traveller-friendly is Line 2 – glide between the Nieuwe Kerk (New Church), a fragrant flower market, Van Gogh Museum and vast Vondelpark, the city's green lungs. However, true trolleybus junkies need a different route to reach the Electrisch Tram Museum, where rides on vintage streetcars recapture a flavour of old-school Amsterdam.

The best time to visit Amsterdam is May (for tulips) and August (for the most reliable sunshine).

✪ DOUGLAS, ISLE OF MAN

Public transport doesn't often halt for hay breaks – unless you're on Douglas' promenade, a 3km seafront serviced by the world's oldest surviving horse-drawn tram. It's not a high-speed option; these open-sided carriages, hauled along narrow-gauge tracks by redoubtable equine engines, stop frequently along the prom (stick out your arm to hail the tram, and pat the pony powering it). However, dating back to 1876, it's the most historical way to traverse the Isle of Man's minuscule capital. Once you've been taken for a ride, head to the Home of Rest for Old Horses to see where these magnificent 'motors' retire.

The Rest Home in Richmond Hill, Douglas, has a museum, cafe and more than 60 horses. See www.iom-horseshome.com.

✪ KIMBERLEY, SOUTH AFRICA

South Africa isn't big on trams. But it *is* big on holes. Really big. And in Kimberley, epicentre of the Karoo's

diamond-mining industry, you can use an elegant example of one to reach a mindboggling instance of the other. Every hour a vintage, 1913 streetcar trundles between Kimberley's City Hall and – well, for want of a better name – the Big Hole. This 214m-deep, 1.6km-perimeter pit is allegedly the largest ever excavated by hand, hacked out since 1871 by pick-wielding prospectors. Riding there by tram – rather than more modern transportation – seems a fitting nod to their low-tech achievement.

The Big Hole is open 8am to 5pm daily; guided tours run on the hour from 9am. Allow three to four hours to visit. See www.thebighole.co.za.

✪ HONG KONG

Often confused with the Peak Tram – a tourist-magnet funicular that's been hauling sunset-sightseers heavenwards since 1888 – Hong Kong's real treat is the similarly historical (but horizontal) charmer that clanks its leisurely way along the island's northern shore. Linking Kennedy Town with Shau Kei Wan, the first electric vehicles traversed this route in 1904; it's now the world's only wooden-sided double-decker tramline. Drop your HK$2 coin (US$0.25) in the slot by the driver, shimmy up the narrow spiral stairway, bag a front-row, top-deck seat and trundle between the narrow, stall-lined cut-throughs, space-age skyscrapers, squawking markets and steaming noodle bars.

Trams run every few minutes between 6am and midnight; the longest ride takes about 1½ hours.

THE WORLD'S
FINEST FREEBIES

IT SOUNDS TOO GOOD TO BE TRUE – BUT THESE TOP-CLASS
EXPERIENCES WON'T COST YOU A PENNY.

01 STATEN ISLAND FERRY, NEW YORK, USA

Cruises usually cost a packet. OK, this one only lasts 25 minutes, and there's no quoits or cocktail lounge (though there is a bar selling beer). But it doesn't cost a cent. Ferries have connected Staten Island and lower Manhattan since the 18th century. Today's tangerine-bright boats have become NYC icons; one, the *Spirit of America,* is part-made of steel salvaged from the Twin Towers. And though the World Trade Center is now missing, the view of the New York skyline – shrinking as you pitch across the bay, and looming large as you return – is still world class.
Ferries run 24 hours daily, from South Ferry at Battery Park. See www.siferry.com.

02 LOUVRE, PARIS, FRANCE

Simply, it's the greatest collection of art ever assembled, displayed in a building that is both a typical Parisian palace and a strikingly modern pyramid of glass. There are over 35,000 items in this matchless repository, from ancient Egyptian antiquities to Greek treasures, Persian trinkets and paintings spanning countries and centuries. Its depth and breadth is overwhelming; you really need more than a day. But if that's all you have, make it a certain day: on the first Sunday of the month, the Louvre is free – something, surely, to make even the resident Mona Lisa crack a proper smile.
The Louvre is open daily except Tuesday from 9am to 6pm (to 10pm Wednesday and Friday); regular admission costs €10 (US$14.40). See www.louvre.fr.

03 CITY BIKES, COPENHAGEN, DENMARK

Copenhagen is the two-wheeled capital of the world: every day 37% of locals cycle to work, and there are 390km of dedicated cycle lanes. So really, it would be rude not to join in – a gesture made all the easier by Bycyklen, the city's free bike scheme. Stacked at racks around central Copenhagen, these complimentary cycles are the perfect way to get around the blissfully flat capital. You can pedal from the cafes lining the brightly painted harbourfront to hippie-hangout Christiania, the kitsch-but-cool Tivoli Gardens and around the grounds of 17th-century Rosenborg Castle – without it costing a single krona.
A 20 krona coin is needed to release a bike, which is refunded when you return it. Bikes are available from March or April to November; see www.bycyklen.dk.

❂ TSIM SHA TSUI WATERFRONT, HONG KONG

It's two for the price of none on the Tsim Sha Tsui waterfront. This promenade at the tip of Kowloon hugs Victoria Harbour; it's where modern shopping centres meet the old colonial Clock Tower, and where the Star Ferry chugs in. It's also where, three mornings a week, t'ai chi gurus Mr Ng and Ms Wu lead free sessions of this meditative martial art against a backdrop of Hong Kong Island's just-distant skyscrapers. Revisit at night for something less subtle, as the Symphony of Lights laser-sound spectacular sets the high rises a-sparkle, Tsim Sha Tsui offers the best seat in the house.

T'ai chi lessons run from 8am to 9am on Monday, Wednesday and Friday. The light show starts at 8pm daily. See www .discoverhongkong.com.

❂ WALKING TOUR, REYKJAVÍK, ICELAND

Iceland sure ain't cheap. Despite the economic meltdown, this almost-Arctic island is still going to test your bank balance. So freebies here taste all the sweeter – and Goecco's Reykjavik Free Tours are as unique and feisty as a shot of *brennivín* (the local firewater – drink with caution...). These two-hour easy ambles around the secret sites of Reykjavík are led by 'performance historians'. You'll see the city's maritime architecture, historical foundations, coolest districts and best bathing spots, accompanied by lashings of Icelandic quirk – stories told

MARTIN LLADO » LPI

GET ON YER BIKE – IT'S FREE IN COPENHAGEN

with actorly verve, which lift the lid on this inscrutable capital.

Tours depart Ingolfs Square at 1pm Monday to Saturday, from 15 May to 1 October. See www.goecco.com.

✪ TEA, GRAND BAZAAR, ISTANBUL, TURKEY

Pyramids of spices waft their pungent scents and cabinets of gold glitter and dazzle. Lanterns dangle, ceramics teeter and tourist tat triumphs – İstanbul's Grand Bazaar is a retail blitzkrieg, an undercover labyrinth of endless stuff. Browsing the stalls is wonderful but exhausting, as is fending off a harem of eager shopkeepers. So give in and let the carpet-seller with the best lines lead you into his showroom, then sip small glasses of apple tea while roll upon roll of woven flooring is unfurled before you with hopeful theatrics and persuasive spiel. It's İstanbul's most atmospheric freebie – as long as the salesman isn't too convincing…

The Grand Bazaar is open 9am to 7pm Monday to Saturday. Take a tram to Beyazit, Üniversite or Sirkeci.

✪ TE PAPA TONGAREWA, WELLINGTON, NEW ZEALAND

See all of New Zealand for nothing at Te Papa. Well, sort of – this beefy building on Wellington's waterfront is the country's national museum, where you'll find its finest art, its history brought to life, and its Maori culture explained and celebrated. Given the wide remit, the gems inside are unsurprisingly eclectic – from *pounamu* (greenstone) clubs to stuffed kiwis, and from a pair of prosthetic cycling legs to a 1.4 billion-year-old stone. To learn about the Maori, start with the Treaty of Waitangi display, then visit the *marae,* a modern take on the traditional meeting house, designed to be used by all cultures.

Te Papa is open daily, including public holidays, from 10am to 6pm (to 9pm Thurs). See www.tepapa.govt.nz.

✪ REICHSTAG, BERLIN, GERMANY

If only these walls could talk…they'd probably talk of walls. Not to mention suspected arson, air raids, Nazi zeal and ignominious decay – the German Parliament building has seen it all since its completion in 1894. But since the fall of Berlin's infamous city-slicing concrete barrier, the Reichstag has risen as dramatically as the eagle on the German flag. Architect Norman Foster masterminded a glorious resurrection, icing the 'new' edifice with a gleaming glass-and-steel cupola, commanding brilliant Berlin views. Best of all? A tour of all this history – including access to the all-seeing dome itself – is absolutely free.

Reichstag tours must be booked in advance; send your preferred time and date to besucherdienst@bundestag.de.

✪ TOKYO METROPOLITAN GOVERNMENT BUILDING, JAPAN

It can be tough to get your head around Tokyo; it's the most populous city in the world, a seething megapolis of over 30 million people rushing between canyons of skyscrapers. Get some perspective by looking down on it from 202m up – for free. The observatory of the Metropolitan

JOHN SONES » LPI

Government Building looms amid high-rise Shinjuku, the district for gadget-shopping and bar-hopping (Shinjuku's 'Golden Gai' is a tumble-down shantytown of over 200 bars). Ascend the elevator to the 45th floor of the North Observatory to see the urban chaos below and, on a clear day, distant Mt Fuji making a stand for Mother Nature.

The North Observatory has a cafe and bar, and is open 9.30am to 11pm daily. See www.metro.tokyo.jp.

✪ ROYAL OPERA HOUSE LUNCHTIME CONCERTS, LONDON, ENGLAND

A Tube ticket might cost a small fortune in the British capital, but it's amazing how much there is to do for nowt. Some of the world's best museums – such as the Natural History, the Victoria & Albert and the British – show-off their incredible collections for nothing. But for an even grander spectacle (and a glimpse of a world traditionally reserved for those with bigger budgets) head to Covent Garden's Royal Opera House on a Monday lunchtime. This classical portico-fronted theatre, completed in 1858, runs special recitals, allowing cheapskates to hear top pianists tinkle and baritones bellow without paying a penny.

Some tickets can be reserved online nine days prior to a concert; some are released from 10am on the day. See www.roh.org.uk.

BEST PLACES FOR
INTREPID
ROMANTICS

PARIS IS PASSE! SHOW HOW ORIGINAL YOUR LOVE IS BY WHISKING YOUR PARTNER AWAY TO AN OFF-BEAT BUT LOVED-UP LOCATION.

01 CAPRI, ITALY

The island where Ulysses was seduced by the singing sirens seems to sprinkle fairy dust over all who come. Capri has captured the hearts of visitors from the Roman Emperor Tiberius to British novelist Graham Greene, and inspired Pablo Neruda to write a whole collection of love poetry during his stay. This Cupid-like isle offers enough chi-chi dining, dramatically dizzying cliff views and ancient ruins to cast a rose-tinted haze over any holiday. Love will definitely be in the air when you whisk your other half off to visit the crumbling remnants of Villa Jovis and then surprise them with a picnic along the south coast's Pizzolungo trail.

With its central location in Anacapri, the historic Casa Mariantonia hotel is the ideal spot for a couple's getaway. See www .casamariantonia.com.

02 WEST COAST, SOUTH ISLAND, NEW ZEALAND

The poignant love triangle of the film *The Piano,* with its storyline of unrequited, forbidden and lustful love, found a perfectly moody counterpart in its setting among the raw and rugged landscape of New Zealand's wild West Coast. With its windswept, driftwood-strewn beaches, secluded lakes and tracts of native forest, all backed by the mighty Southern Alps, this region's unspoiled charms are perfect for nature-loving couples planning a passionate tryst far from the rat race. Top your holiday off with a stop in the greenstone-capital of Hokitika to pick out a jade memento for your partner.

The luxury Lake Brunner Lodge is the West Coast's premier historic hotel. See www.lakebrunner.co.nz.

03 BYBLOS, LEBANON

All cobblestone souqs and blooming bougainvilleas, even the Egyptian gods chose Byblos as the perfect place for a romantic rendezvous. Local mythology relates it was here that the goddess Isis was finally reunited with her partner Osiris, bringing him back to life after his murder by jealous Seth. Today the pristinely preserved old town is still a starry-eyed lover's delight. Once a grand Phoenician port, these days the narrow

WALTER BIBIKOW » PHOTOLIBRARY

alleys that wind higgledy-piggledy down to the sea exude a distinctly laid-back air. For coupledom heaven, grab a table harbour-side and indulge in a candle-lit dinner complete with slowly sipped cocktails as sunset sweeps across the Mediterranean.
The King's Well is where, according to legend, Isis wept for Osiris. It's inside Byblos' archaeological site, which is open daily 8am to 5pm; admission is LBP6000 (US$4).

✪ CARTAGENA, COLOMBIA

It's no wonder Gabriel Garcia Marquez set his passionate novel of obsession, *Love in the Time of Cholera*, in Cartagena – this tropically sultry city simply oozes Caribbean city-break chic. During the day stroll hand-in-hand through the streets of Ciudad Amarullada (the walled colonial city) where candy-coloured mansions with balconies overflowing with flowers are a culture-vulture couple's dream. But it's when the sun goes down that this city really sizzles. Unashamedly sexy, Cartagena's colourful nightlife will have you and your loved one salsa-ing happily into the future together.
The charming Alfiz Boutique Hotel is a cosy choice for a romantic break. See www.alfizhotel.com.

✪ RUHUNA YALA NATIONAL PARK, SRI LANKA

Maybe it's the added fizz of adrenaline from being out in the wild together, but there's always been a whiff of romance about wildlife safaris. In the south of Sri Lanka, this national park boasts some of the best leopard-spotting in the world, as well as a wealth of other animal and birdlife. For extra relationship brownie points, don't forget to woo your partner with Ruhuna Yala's own happy-ever-after legend. This is where Kaayantissa, King of Ruhuna, first met and fell in love with the Princess Vihara Maha Devi after he found her, washed up ashore, having bravely sacrificed herself for her people.

January to May is the best time for wildlife-spotting; the park usually closes between mid-August and mid-October.

✪ KHAJURAHO, MADHYA PRADESH, INDIA

The Chandela Rhajputs obviously knew a thing or two about the importance of lovemaking in a relationship, and it's obvious that prudish sculptors were not required when it came to decorating their temples. This medieval Indian dynasty's cultural capital is extravagantly decorated with erotic art – just the ticket if you and your spouse are looking to add some spice to your relationship. It's best viewed in the early morning, when the soft buttery yellow of the sandstone seems to glow in the light; head to the Khandariya-Mahadev Temple in the Western Enclosure to see the most lavish of the carvings.

From Delhi the overnight sleeper train to Khajuraho leaves at 8.15pm six times per week, arriving at 6.50am.

✪ KAYAKÖY, TURKEY

This enchanting spot was the inspiration for Louis de Bernières's *Birds Without Wings,* where the novel's doomed love affair between Ibrahim the Goatherd and Philothei the Beautiful was played out. Only a short journey from the popular resort of Fethiye, Kayaköy is a rural idyll set snugly between splendidly lush rolling hills – just right for lovers looking for a rustic hideaway. Spreading over the hillside above the hamlet are the haunting ruins of the abandoned Greek village, which was deserted during Turkey's population exchange. Explore these evocative reminders of a lost community before getting both your hearts pounding by trekking the section of the Lycian Way that begins from here.

In the centre of the village, Poseidon Restaurant is an intimate venue for dinner, specialising in old Ottoman and Greek dishes.

✪ IZUMO-TAISHA SHRINE, IZUMO, JAPAN

Couples flock to Japan's oldest shrine to ask the Shinto god of marriage, Okuninushi, to bless their relationship. This daring deity stole the heart of Suserihime, daughter of the god of the underworld, and whisked her away from her father's lair, earning his grudging admiration. Every October all the Shinto gods, are believed to descend here to discuss the year's forthcoming marriages. To assure health and happiness in your relationship, throw a coin into the offering box, say a short prayer and clap four times – twice for yourself and twice for your beloved.

From Izumo Station, the Ichibata Dentetsu train line takes about 20 minutes to Izumo-Taisha-Mai Station; the shrine is nearby.

❂ PRINCE EDWARD ISLAND, CANADA

The scene of every little girl's childhood literary crush, Canada's smallest province is a cosy countryside escape of pastoral rolling hills and vast stretches of sandy beaches. It was here that LM Montgomery's most beloved character, the freckle-faced orphan Anne-with-an-E Shirley of Green Gables, fell in love with ultimate boy next door Gilbert Blythe. Hire bicycles and ride over the red-clay roads of this tranquil island enclave together and finish with a visit to Green Gables itself, which provided the inspiration for this enduring love story.

Green Gables is open daily to visitors from May to October (9am to 5pm). Personalised tours are available; for details see www.gov.pe.ca/greengables.

❂ SALZBURG, AUSTRIA

Mature-aged couples have always been partial to Salzburg's charms, but the cheese factor of the *Sound of Music* connection has had a tendency to put off the younger generation. It's time to put this city of church spires and baroque architecture back on the loved-up holiday radar. Wander the craftsman-lined lane of Linzergasse, take in the tranquil atmosphere of St Sebastian Church and admire the majesty of Salzburg Dom. The hills may well be alive with the sound of music, but Salzburg has much more to offer romantic city-breaks than singing nuns.

Drink a stein together at the famous Müllner Bräu beer garden. Buy a token and then join the queue to be served beer directly from the barrel.

RICCARDO SPILA » 4CORNERS IMAGES

PLAN A PASSIONATE TRYST FAR FROM THE RAT RACE ON LAKE MATHESON, SOUTH ISLAND, NEW ZEALAND

BEST PLACES TO FIND
MIDDLE EARTH

PACK YOUR BAGGINS AND LOOK OUT FOR HOBBITS, ELVES AND DWARVES IN PLACES OUT OF JRR TOLKIEN'S FICTIONAL WORLD.

01 PACAYA, GUATEMALA

Probably way off Tolkien's radar, the Pacaya volcano in Guatemala does have some similar features to Mount Doom in Mordor. Pacaya first erupted some 23,000 years ago and has been continuously pumping out sulphuric gas since 1965. Easily reached by bus from the nearby city of Antigua, Pacaya is a popular two-hour climb to the top. The panoramic views above the clouds are astonishing and you can almost ski your way down on the ash.

The Vila Flor Hotel (www.vilaflorhotel .com) in nearby Antigua offers tours to the volcanoes and a fine cup of locally grown Guatemalan coffee.

02 PENDLE HILL, ENGLAND

It is thought that Tolkien found his inspiration for hobbits in the woods of the Ribble Valley. This mystical part of Lancashire is dominated by Pendle Hill, a dark shape isolated from the Pennines like the fictional Lonely Mountain. The names of places here have a fairy-tale feel – the Forest of Bowland, the River Ribble and Wolfhole Crag – to name just a few. Pendle is also famous for its medieval witchcraft, and hikers can walk along the Pendle Witches Trail. But it's not all black magic –

George Fox, founder of the Quakers, was also spellbound by the hill.

Pendle Hill is best reached from the village of Barley. For information on hiking and biking tours see www.visitlancashire.com.

03 ROCAMADOUR, FRANCE

Uncannily similar to the fictional 'White City' of Minas Tirith in Gondor, scene of the pivotal Battle of the Pelennor Fields, Rocamadour rises from the scraggly limestone cliffs overlooking a deep gorge alongside the River Alzou. They say truth is stranger than fiction, and if local legend is to be believed then Rocamadour was founded by a hermit who was guided here by an angel. A place of Christian pilgrimage since medieval times, devotees can climb the 233 steps of the Great Staircase or take a lift to the shrine.

Rocamadour is off the A20 motorway, 100 km north of Toulouse; see www .tourisme-lot.com.

✪ MATAMATA, NEW ZEALAND

You don't have to be a Tolkien geek to enjoy Matamata, but most people that come to this rural town on the North Island are hunting for hobbits. Matamata is home to Hobbiton, the film set of *The Lord of the Rings*. When director Peter

BARBARA VAN ZANTEN » LPI

Jackson came across Alexander Farm, he knew he'd found the perfect location for The Shire. After filming was completed, the government decided to keep the hobbit holes, though visitors today are more likely to see grazing sheep rather than characters like Frodo, Merry and Pippin – never mind the dreaded Nazgûl. *Alexander Farm is located on Buckland Rd, Matamata. Tours run from Auckland, Tauranga and Hamilton; see www.hobbit ontours.com.*

✪ GREAT SMOKY MOUNTAINS, USA
They don't call them the Smokies for nothing. This giant mountain range, stretching 2108km through North Carolina and Tennessee, is known for its fog – just like the Misty Mountains in Middle Earth. The Smokies were the homeland of the Cherokee tribe, the majority of whom were forced west by the *Indian Removal Act* of 1830 (or 'Trail of Tears'). Today it's the most-visited national park in the USA, offering outdoor activities including camping, fishing and horse riding. *Around 1500 black bears live in the park, as do salamanders, elk and white-tailed deer. For detailed information on wildlife and more, see www.nps.gov/grsm.*

✪ STROMBOLI, ITALY
Off the northern coast of Sicily, the island of Stromboli is home to one of the most active volcanoes on earth. In fact, geologists use the term 'Strombolian' to describe violent eruptions in other countries. Not surprisingly, this fiery island is said to be the inspiration for Orodruin, the fiery mountain of Mordor, in the land of the Dark Lord Sauron. Although it has been spurting out molten rock from its lava crater without break since 1932, Stromboli is still widely visited, but only 800 (quite brave) people live there. *Minutes from the volcano and Stromboli's harbour, the Ossidiana Hotel (www .hotelossidiana.it) is for those wanting to be close to the action.*

✪ DRAKENSBERG, SOUTH AFRICA
Literally translated as 'Dragon Mountain' in Dutch, Drakensberg sounds and looks like something out of folklore. An immense and remote mountainous wonderland, it is as vast as Middle Earth itself. The Zulus call Drakensberg 'uKhahlamba' ('Barrier of Spears') as it creates a natural border between Lesotho and the KwaZulu-Natal region. Lodges and base camps are scattered across this UNESCO World Heritage site, home to over 290 species of birds and 48 species of mammals. *The only way to reach Drakensberg is via the Sani Pass, which is some 3000m high at its peak. For maps and more, see www .kzn.org.za.*

✪ STIRLING CASTLE, SCOTLAND
Sitting atop a hill of solid volcanic rock that was forced up from deep within the earth millions of years ago, Stirling Castle has been notoriously difficult to attack. Like Tolkien's Helm's Deep (site of the Battle of the Hornburg), Stirling is set in a strong naturally defensive position, a good spot to shoot arrows at invading Orcs (or, for preference, Englishmen). A symbol of Scottish pride, the castle has witnessed the victories of William Wallace

and Robert the Bruce, though most of the buildings at Stirling today date from the 15th and 16th centuries.

Stirling Castle opens from 9am to 5pm in winter and 9am to 6pm in summer; find more at www.stirlingcastle.gov.uk.

✪ REDWOOD NATIONAL PARK, USA

OK, the trees found in Redwood National Park in California can't walk or talk like the Ents of the deadly fictional forests of Mirkwood and Fangorn, but they are the tallest specimens in the world. Aside from trees, Redwood also has crystal-clear streams, prairies and 64km of wild coastline. The coastal redwood trees generally live for 500 to 700 years and a few are said to be 2000 years old, making them some of the oldest living things on earth (apart from wizards, of course).

Redwood National Park has five information centres open daily from 9am to 6pm (summer), 9am to 5pm (spring) and 9am to 4pm (winter). For details go to www. nps.gov/redw.

✪ LAUTERBRUNNEN VALLEY, SWITZERLAND

You don't need to stretch your imagination too far to pretend that this corner of Switzerland is actually Rivendell, the realm of the Elves and site of the Council of Elrond, where Frodo accepted his fate as Ring-bearer. Tolkien actually travelled here in 1919 and his painting of Rivendell looks much like Lauterbrunnen, with its deep, lush valley with waterfalls set against the backdrop of snowy mountains. Located in the canton of Bern, the valley is dotted with villages such as Grindelwald and Wengen, and is a popular spot for winter sports.

Wengen is one of the few car-free resorts in Europe and is served by the Wengernalpbahn railway. For train timetables see www.sbb.ch.

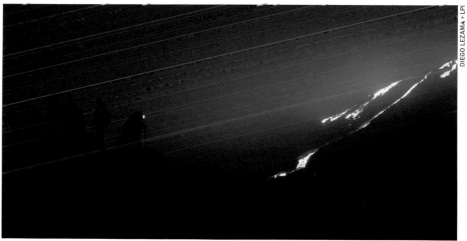

DON'T TRY THIS AT HOME – LAVA FLOW AT PACAYA VOLCANO, GUATEMALA

DIEGO LEZAMA ▸ LPI

GREATEST RACES
TO WATCH LIVE

WATCH SCUTTLING CRABS, GALLOPING CAMELS AND THE
WORLD'S FASTEST SNAILS – ALL WITHOUT BREAKING A SWEAT.

01 TOUR DE FRANCE FINISH, CHAMPS-ÉLYSÉES, PARIS

So much for time trials and mountain stages, for sheer pageantry, nothing in the world of cycling beats the grand finale of its greatest race when, having ridden 3500km across the length and breadth of France, riders put the pedal to the metal down Paris' most prestigious street. Strangely enough, the overall winner of race has usually been decided well before the riders reach Paris (often on the notoriously steep Alpe d'Huez stage) so the Paris stage simply formalises the result. However, there are still points available for the sprinters, so a fast finish is guaranteed. With ample opportunity to see your favourite cyclists up close, the atmosphere – bustling cafes, jostling fans and frantic French commentary – is unforgettable.

Several tour operators offer the chance for nonprofessionals to ride parts of the tour: try Custom Getaways (www.custom getaways.com).

02 CAMEL RACING, DUBAI

Sand-storming up in the popularity stakes across the Emirates is this age-old sport, enjoying a renaissance thanks to the bizarre intervention of robots (no, you didn't misread that). As if the ancient sight of camels stampeding across sand against a starkly modern urban skyline wasn't juxtaposition enough, now, US$25,000 tailor-made robotic jockeys ride the animals round the racetrack in place of the young children (which had the sport swamped in controversy), while owners remotely control them from 4WDs speeding alongside. Fans say camel racing has never been so exciting, as the machines weigh the camels down less than children. But robots can malfunction and camels are temperamental beasts...

Dubai's new Al Lisaili camel racetrack is on the Al Ain road at Exit 37, past the Rugby Sevens Stadium. Race times are usually 6am Thursday to Sunday, November to March.

03 GOAT & CRAB RACING FESTIVAL, BUCCOO, TOBAGO

It all started back in 1925 as the regular Tobagans' reaction to the wealthy colonialists' sport of racing thoroughbred horses in neighbouring Trinidad. Today, Easter Tuesday's goat race at Buccoo, a fishing village in Tobago's secluded southwest, has achieved cult status. The comical race, in which competitors run behind their bleating steeds, is the focal point to a brilliant collage of events, including a goat parade with commentary and a major sideshow in the equally competitive sport of crab racing (don't ask). It's all set on the cusp of vibrant Buccoo Reef, home to some 40 coral species.

Recover from the revelry at Arnos Vale Hotel (www.arnosvalehotel.com), a former sugar plantation set in 450 acres of tantalising tropical grounds.

✪ COAST TO COAST, NEW ZEALAND

Combining running, cycling and kayaking, this gruelling 243km traverse from the east to west coasts of New Zealand's South Island – crossing the Southern Alpine mountains in the process – is touted as the planet's toughest adventure race. For spectators it offers stunning scenery, with the 66km kayak down the wild Waimarkariri River, rapids and all, regarded as the race highlight, especially where the water funnels into an imposing gorge, with ice-capped peaks looming above. The route is riddled with oddly-familiar scenery, too: many of the iconic shots in Peter Jackson's Lord of the Rings trilogy were filmed hereabouts.

Find out more about the Speight's Coast to Coast at www.coasttocoast.co.nz

CHRISTOPHE FARABA »CORBIS

PEDAL PUSHING, PARIS STYLE – TOUR DE FRANCE

SNAIL RACING, NORFOLK, UK

...eady, steady, slow: so goes the catchphrase at the leading competitive snail-racing venue, a cricket pitch in the sedate Norfolk village of Congham. It doesn't provide many adrenaline highs (unless you're a participating gastropod), but compensates for that in sheer surreality as crowds gather to glimpse the snails (marked for identification purposes) race from the centre of a table to its periphery under the watchful eye of the 'snailmaster'. Why Congham? It has lots of ponds around, apparently. Snails like ponds.

The best nearby digs are at Congham Hall (www.conghamhallhotel.co.uk), a luxurious Georgian manor, estate and herb garden with log fires and a spa.

✪ GREAT AMAZON RAFT RACE, PERU

Ever wondered how you could rock up at a city of 500,000 people when there are no access roads? This annual jungle raft race to Iquitos may not quite be what you envisaged, but hundreds of crews in weird and wonderful vessels have taken to the world's greatest river to give the event a go. This stretch of the Amazon is transformed into a cornucopia of colourful crafts (built by competing teams from scratch before launch) contending with caimans, piranhas, currents and each other in order to complete the 180km course.

Take your own trip on the Amazon in a hand-built riverboat with Dawn On The Amazon (www.dawnontheamazon.com) who also provide raft race information.

INSY SHAH » GETTY IMAGES

ROBOTS, BELIEVE IT OR NOT, HAVE REVIVED THE SPORT OF CAMEL RACING IN DUBAI

✪ THE GREAT RENO BALLOON RACE, USA

Every September for the last 35 years or so, the skies above Reno have become a blaze of ballooning glory. With three days of races, displays and challenges, this technicolour event – the largest free ballooning meet in the USA – wows some 140,000 spectators, as pilots compete for a US$20,000 first prize. But the high-altitude fun doesn't end with a simple race; also on offer is 'Balloon Blackjack', and Reno's famous 'Hare and Hounds' event, an airborne simulation of a traditional British hunt, during which 100 balloons chase down two hot-air 'hares', provided by the Wells Fargo Bank. Bank managers spouting hot air will never seem the same again.

The festival takes to the skies for three days each September; visit www.reno balloon.com for more details.

✪ MONGOL DERBY, MONGOLIA

If you really want to feel like a latter-day Marco Polo, experiencing this 1000km unsignposted romp through the Mongolian steppe is the way to do it. Far and away the world's most arduous horse race, the derby sees entrants saddling up in much the same manner as the famed explorer did eight centuries ago, carrying all their gear and refuelling at homes of local families en route. It will just be you, your steed, your GPS (in case you get lost, which is incredibly easy) and kilometre after kilometre of remote, rolling plains.

Zavkhan (www.zavkhan.co.uk) is a New Zealand–Mongolian outfit specialising in exploring remote regions of Mongolia by horse.

✪ DAKAR RALLY, CHILE & ARGENTINA

A rally based around a Frenchman getting lost while on a rally...hmm. Despite having switched from the original France–Senegal route to South American Patagonia, this legendary race is most definitely still on the radar of serious off-road race enthusiasts, with trucks, bikes, quad bikes and cars converging to career across thousands of kilometres of the most rugged terrain around. Adventure hot spot Patagonia has thrown tracts of the Andes and swaths of the driest desert on Earth into the path of participants, alongside an enviable palette – from the lush greens of the pampas to the fiery reds of the Atacama at sunset – beckoning over the course of this 13-day odyssey.

Get the low-down on rallies past and future at www.dakar.com.

✪ BADWATER ULTRAMARATHON, CALIFORNIA, USA

Taking its superfit participants from 85m below sea level to 2530m above in a mere 217km, the Badwater course is every bit as 'bad' as its name suggests. The world's toughest road-running race gives entrants just 48 hours to make it from the depths of Death Valley, the lowest point in the western hemisphere, up to the slopes of Mt Whitney, one of the USA's highest points. It's an arresting part of the planet; salt flats, dunes, canyons and monumental mountain ranges are all part of the package.

Explore the wilderness of Death Valley (www.nps.gov/deva) in which the race unfolds; guided hikes taking in the geology and wildlife are available.

P
007 DESTINATIONS

BEAT BOND TO PARADISE WITH A SORTIE INTO HIS MOST ENVIABLE SOJOURNS OF THE LAST HALF-CENTURY – YOU'LL BE SHAKEN AND STIRRED BY THE RESULTS

01 KHAO PHING KAN, PHUKET, THAILAND

This self-styled 'James Bond Island' comes courtesy of *The Man with a Golden Gun,* the latter scenes of which were filmed in Thailand (Khao Phing Kan is baddy Scaramanga's hideaway in the film). Back in 1974 when the film was shot, the island was an undiscovered paradise. Now tourists flock by the busload, but the place is still idyllic, if completely devoid of almost anything tangibly Bond-related. Still, several other jungle-topped limestone promontories – which Bond would have obligingly skinny-dipped off – also rear out of the turquoise water hereabouts. Guess where everyone else isn't.

Outdo the day trippers with a serene sunset cruise to the islands of Phang Nga Bay on a Scaramanga-esque junk with June Bahtra (www.phuket-travel.com/cruises).

02 PRAGUE, CZECH REPUBLIC

In a film series with West–East rivalry as a core theme, it would be wrong not to give the Communist Bloc a mention, and Prague was the first Bond locale behind the old Iron Curtain to be used as an actual setting. It is here in the 2006 remake of *Casino Royale* that a new-look Bond, played by a gritty Daniel Craig, gains his licence to kill. Plenty of city landmarks make a appearance, including the lavish baroque library of gorgeous Strahov Monastery. Karlovy Vary, a sedate old spa town in the country's northwest, stands in as the Casino Royale itself.

Wander rooms almost a millennium old and gaze upon ancient texts at the monastery. See www.strahovskyklaster.cz.

03 OCHO RIOS, JAMAICA

Those lucky citizens of Ocho Rios – of all the towns in all the world, Ursula Andress walked into theirs, and then into film legend. On the evidence of *Dr No,* she spent her most memorable moments nearby on the lovely Laughing Waters beach, and only in her bikini, too. Her screen entrance here puts Halle Berry's similarly scantily clad introduction in *Die Another Day* (and, indeed, almost every other subsequent Bond moment) into the shade. But it gets better for Bond fans. The spy's creator Ian Fleming built his dream villa just along the coast, and the inspiration for the secret agent's capers was purportedly gleaned here.

Stay at Fleming's villa (www.goldeneye .com), complete with its own private pool

STEVE VIDLER » PHOTOLIBRARY

and barbecuing spots at secret coves
within the grounds.

⊙ NASSAU, BAHAMAS

What hasn't Bond done in the Bahamas?
Films from *Thunderball* to *Casino Royale*
have been shot in this dreamy chain of
islands, which for many represent paradise
personified: palm-fringed beaches,
glamorous waterfront bars, celebrity
residents and even the odd casino. But
colonial capital Nassau, with its past

history of piracy and luxuriant debauchery,
seems to be 007's favourite haunt. The
precedent was set when the city's One
& Only Ocean club starred in the original
Casino Royale. If you walk around today,
there's every chance you'll encounter
someone with their very own Bond story,
plucked from the filming of spy-related
antics here over the past 50 years.
Learn to dive with the man who instructed
Sean Connery in Never Say Never Again
(www.stuartcove.com).

✪ MIAMI, FLORIDA, USA

Remember when Jill Masterson is covered in gold paint and asphyxiated by Oddjob in *Goldfinger*, and Goldfinger himself cheats at cards? Arguably the Bond franchise's best-ever sequence came courtesy of Miami's Fontainebleau Hotel – or its Pinewood Studios mock-up. Florida also plays a less-touted yet still more crucial part in the films, too: up at Silver Springs is where many underwater Bond moments were shot, most notably those in *Thunderball* and *Moonraker*.

Follow in the footsteps of countless celebrities and book into the Fontainebleau yourself (www.fontainebleau.com).

✪ LONDON, UK

What? No sun, casinos or beaches? Perhaps not, but without Pinewood Studios all bar one Bond films would not have existed. Then there's the headquarters of the Secret Intelligence Service (aka MI6) at Vauxhall, a hugely impressive building actually used as a location in all Bond films since *GoldenEye*. Last but not least, further down the River Thames in London's East End is where the opening boat chase scene of *The World Is Not Enough* took place. The river's 9mph boat speed limit was broken a few times...

You can delve into 007's London haunts with a spy tour of the capital through Brit Movie Tours (www.britmovietours.com).

✪ HIMEJI CASTLE, HONSHU, JAPAN

The ninja training school in *You Only Live Twice*, Himeji Castle, headed a star cast of iconic Japanese locations for the film. The 17th-century fortress is one of

DOUG MCKINLAY » LPI

IN PRAGUE A NEW-LOOK JAMES BOND (DANIEL CRAIG) GAINS HIS LICENCE TO KILL IN THE 2006 REMAKE OF *CASINO ROYALE*

Japan's finest buildings, with its brilliant white exterior and gracefully curved walls, parapets and roofs resembling an arrangement of oriental fans. It's also the place where 007 turns Japanese (martial arts, disguise, the lot) to discover where the evil Blofeld has his hideout, which (surprise surprise) isn't too far away – in a volcano in Kirishima National Park on Kyushu, in fact. Well, at least until the villain detonates his entire base at the end of the film, that is.

Himeji Castle (www.himeji-castle.gr.jp) is open 9am to 5pm from June to August and 9am to 4pm from September to May

✪ AGHIA TRIADA, METEORA, GREECE

One of five hair-raisingly vertiginous clifftop monasteries in Greece's Kalambaka region, Aghia Triada's selection as a climactic finale in *For Your Eyes Only* didn't wash well with neighboring monks, who reportedly hung dirty washing out in protest at the film crew. Nevertheless, the building became part of one of the most memorable Bond scenes, in which Roger Moore scales the high summit and almost falls to his death when a henchman of arch-villain Kristatos dislodges his crampons To make Moore feel better, the way up was always tough; constructed during 14th-century Serbian–Byzantine wars, the monastery's original access route was via removable ladders that deterred all but the most intrepid. Meteora means 'hovering in the air' – and from afar Aghia Triada appears to do just that.

To get to Meteora take an Athens–Volos train, then connect with the train to Kalambaka the nearest town to the monasteries.

✪ ARECIBO OBSERVATORY, PUERTO RICO

Home to the most original final scene of any Bond flick, Arecibo is better known to 007 devotees as the satellite dish in *GoldenEye* where Pierce Brosnan, stepping into the heroic spy's shoes for the first time, triumphs over and kills defected agent Trevelyan (played by a loathsome Sean Bean). Even when there's no counter-espionage going on, Arecibo, set in remote tree-studded karst hills, hosts the world's largest radio-telescope and has a fascinating museum introducing visitors to the ins and outs of outer space.

Plan your eye-opening visit to Arecibo Observatory at www.naic.edu.

✪ SCHILTHORN, SWITZERLAND

Hats off to Bond's arch-nemesis, Blofeld: the man certainly knew how to pick dramatic spots for his hideaways. The revolving restaurant on this 2900m mountain in the Swiss Alps is his lair for *On Her Majesty's Secret Service*, a film far hotter on location than acting (provided this time by George Lazenby). Filming at the restaurant, which was then not completed, was only allowed on condition that the film company contribute towards construction costs. The Piz Gloria restaurant is still going (and rotating) strong today. You can sample a James Bond buffet and there's even a ski run leading off from here, just like the film. Lazenby would approve.

Ski down Schilthorn like Lazenby in the film or simply enjoy the stunning views from the top. See www.schilthorn.ch.

TITANIC TASTERS

CHANNEL THE SPIRIT OF THE 'UNSINKABLE' SHIP IN 2012, 100 YEARS AFTER ITS INFAMOUS PLUNGE...

01 BELFAST, NORTHERN IRELAND

Belfast was the birthplace of the *Titanic*. In 1909 her keel was laid at its Harland & Wolff shipyard; on 2 April 1912 she sailed from here for Southampton, proud crowds waving off the most luxurious liner the world had seen. But the world has changed, and the city looks different today: the 'Titanic Quarter' is being ambitiously redeveloped, at its heart the new hull-shaped Titanic Belfast attraction, opening in April 2012. But for a more historical take, stroll the slipways from which the vessel was launched, nose into the original H&W offices and gawp at the dry dock – unchanged since *Titanic*'s time – to appreciate the ship's awesome scale.

Two-hour guided walks of Belfast's Titanic Quarter cost £12 (US$19.50). See www .titanicwalk.com.

02 DENVER, COLORADO, USA

They called her 'unsinkable' – not the *Titanic* but Molly Brown. She rose to riches from lowly beginnings after her miner husband struck gold, and went on to survive the *Titanic* tragedy, helping other passengers in the process. But her Denver home almost didn't make it. Threatened with demolition in the 1970s, it was only saved by a group of passionate locals, keen to restore the 19th-century home to its former, Brown-era beauty. Today the Queen Anne–style mansion has been lovingly preserved, and contains a grand staircase, well-stocked library, rich upholstery, elegant piano, chandeliers and silver service to create an opulent 1910s time warp. Molly lives on.

Guided tours of the museum run every 30 minutes from 10am Tuesday to Saturday (Sundays from noon). See www.molly brown.org.

03 CAPE RACE, NEWFOUNDLAND, CANADA

They don't call this 'Iceberg Alley' for nothing. Newfoundland's rugged Atlantic coast is renowned for its glacial goliaths – every year chunks of ice from Greenland float south past the Canadian province. It makes a spectacular sight: big bergs can be spotted from shore, like frozen skyscrapers on the move. But it also makes for treacherous sailing...as the *Titanic* discovered. It was the wireless station at Cape Race – the closest landfall to the wreck site – that first received *Titanic*'s distress call, and relayed the message to the world. Today a wind-whipped lighthouse still warns ships navigating these wild waters.

The best time to spot icebergs is late May to early June; for viewing tips see www .icebergfinder.com.

✪ PIGEON FORGE, TENNESSEE, USA

It's all a little incongruous: a big, ship-shaped museum-monolith sitting an awfully long way from the sea, just down the road from Dollywood and the Dixie Stampede. Nonetheless, Pigeon Forge is home to the world's biggest *Titanic* attraction. It's hands-on stuff: you can shovel coal, patrol the bridge, sit in a life-sized lifeboat and touch an iceberg. Alternatively ransack the gift shop, where there's no need to mount an expedition for priceless diamonds – a 'Heart of the Ocean' necklace (like the trinket from the 1997 Oscar-sweeping *Titanic* film) can be yours for just US$129.99. If only Bill Paxton had known...

Self-guided tours of Titanic Pigeon Forge (open daily) take around two hours. See www.titanicattraction.com.

✪ MELBOURNE, AUSTRALIA

Class discrimination circa 1912 is alive and well at Melbourne's most doomed dining experience. Book a table in steerage at the shipshape Titanic Theatre Restaurant and you eat with the other cheapskates; upgrade to First Class and

A CENTURY OF LEGENDS BEGAN HERE IN BELFAST

JOHN SONES » LPI

RICHARD CUMMINS »LPI

you chink china with a more elite crowd (well, those who paid the extra dollars for posher nosh). Either way, catastrophe is guaranteed by pudding, although after a bit of iceberg acting action, the ending's actually rewritten – the 'passengers' are saved and you all make it to New York to dance the night away! Well, it's not polite to kill off paying customers.

Places at Titanic Theatre Restaurant start at A$80 (US$85), and costumes and accessories can be hired. See www.titanic.com.au.

✪ HALIFAX, NOVA SCOTIA, CANADA

As the nearest port to the *Titanic*'s sink site, the Nova Scotian city of Halifax was closely involved in the rescue operation. There are more than 100 victims of the disaster buried here, but one grave in Halifax's Fairview Cemetery receives a disproportionate number of mourners.

It's the final resting place of body 227, recovered from the bitter Atlantic by a Canadian cable ship and marked by the simplest of headstones, that attracts most attention – because it says 'J Dawson'. *Titanic* movie director James Cameron insists his Jack Dawson was unrelated, but that hasn't stopped Leo DiCaprio lovers paying their movie-inspired respects.

Halifax's Maritime Museum, which contains a Titanic section, is open from 9.30am daily (except Monday November to April). See www.museum.gov.ns.ca.

✪ NEW YORK, USA

The *Titanic* never made it to New York, and neither did Ida Straus – she chose to go down with the ship and her beloved husband Isador. But they reside in their intended destination to this day, in spirit at least. Tiny, triangular Straus Park, on Manhattan's Upper West Side, is a poignant, peaceful tribute. Here, a reclining female bronze gazes into a pool of water, shrouded by crab apples, azaleas and lilies, and scampered upon by squirrels. It's a far cry from Id's other NYC legacy: the Straus-owned Macy's. Head to the hefty department store for a more manic memorial experience.

To reach Straus Park, take Broadway train 1 to 103rd St and Broadway.

⊘ LONG BEACH, CALIFORNIA, USA

Its balmy climes and palmy gardens don't immediately conjure the chill of the mid-Atlantic. But it was in Long Beach – a Hollywood location fave – that the stars of James Cameron's *Titanic* sank or swam, depending on their individual character's fate. The capacious Belmont Olympic Pool provided a safer watery environment for filming, and it's still open to the public for laps and lessons. To get a better feel for big-ship style, wander along the waterfront to the anchored *Queen Mary*. This enormous luxury liner, which crossed the Atlantic 1001 times between 1936 and 1964, is the true grand dame of the ocean.

Belmont Pool (4000 E Olympic Plaza) has 16 lanes, plus diving boards. Admission is US$4.

⊘ SOUTHAMPTON, ENGLAND

Southampton is dotted with statuary commemorating the *Titanic*'s victims: the Musician's Memorial bears the opening bars of a hymn; the Engineer Officers Memorial is a glorious angel; and the memorial to the stewards and firemen sits inside the ruins of Holy Rood Church. The reason for these memorials is that Southampton not only farewelled the *Titanic* on her maiden voyage, but also suffered the greatest losses from her sinking. Of the 1517 people who perished, 549 were from Southampton, virtually all of them crew members. A walk links the memorials, as well as the docks, Maritime Museum and The Grapes pub. The latter was where four would-be *Titanic* sailors made the best mistake of their lives – tarrying too long and missing the boat.

A new Sea City Museum is set to open in Southampton in April 2012, housing Titanic stories and exhibits.

⊘ ORLANDO, FLORIDA, USA

It's no real surprise that Orlando, the motherland of theme parks, has a homage to the world's most famous ship. This isn't quite Titanic-done-Disney (there's no human-sized mouse at the helm, or new happy ending), but the cheese is still chunkily sliced at Florida's Titanic Experience. Actors lead 'passengers' (ie the guests, who are each given a ticket bearing a real *Titanic* traveller's name) onto the 'vessel' to roam replica state rooms and the iconic staircase. It's a bit of fun, but with a poignant finale: guests check their 'name' against the passenger list – to see if they lived or died.

Titanic the Experience is open daily 9am to 9pm; tickets are US$21.95. See www .titanictheexperience.com.

SLEEPING WITH CELEBRITIES

WANT TO BED DOWN WITH THE FAMOUS? COVETING JFK'S SUITE OR CAPONE'S SPEAKEASY TO CRASH IN? CHECK IN TO THE WORLD'S MOST RENOWNED A-LIST ACCOMMODATION.

01 CHELSEA HOTEL, NEW YORK, USA

222 West 23rd Street has had a monumental impact on some of the world's most brilliant and destructive minds, from Bob Dylan and Leonard Cohen (who sang about it) to Arthur Miller (who stayed there after splitting with Marilyn Monroe) and Dylan Thomas (who died there, supposedly after downing 18 successive whiskies). Breakthroughs, break-ups, breakdowns, it's had them all, and in high-octane doses. When one hotel can reel off a list of connections to stardom this long and downright classy, it makes you contemplate whether our current crop of celebrities aren't a tad, well, tame in comparison.
Find out more about the glamorous guests and glamorous rooms at www .hotelchelsea.com.

02 RITZ PARIS, PARIS, FRANCE

'When I dream of afterlife in heaven, the action always takes place at the Ritz Paris,' Ernest Hemingway once said (well, he did get the bar and a suite named after him). Yet a clutch of other celebrities think similarly: Coco Chanel lived at the Ritz for 30 years and authors from Noel Coward to Bret Easton Ellis have set their fiction there. Its legacy doesn't end with the guestbook; back in the 1920s legendary hotel barman Frank Meier decided to write a book on his profession: *The Artistry of Mixing Drinks*. Ninety years on, it's still a bible for bartenders the world over. Salud.
If the Ritz is full, try architecturally eclectic Hotel de Vendôme (www.hotelde vendome.com) down the road, which gives it a close run in the style stakes.

03 HOTEL NACIONAL DE CUBA, HAVANA, CUBA

Cuba was entertaining America's wealthy elite long before the Bahamas or Hawaii, and the Nacional hosted everyone who was anyone before Castro and JFK came along and put the party on ice. As well as Marlon Brando and the country's adopted American son Ernest Hemingway (who donated a fish to the bar), the hotel was a haven for the gangsters that ran amok in Havana in the 1920s and '30s, and the epitome of decadence with the faintest hint of the absolutely corrupt. Still time-trapped in its glam, unaltered pre-Revolution decor, its colossal art deco

JOHN BORTHWICK » LPI

lobby will wow you before the bedrooms even come into view.

Time travel back to Cuba's glory days by booking at www.hotelnacionaldecuba.com.

✪ COPACABANA PALACE, RIO DE JANEIRO, BRAZIL

Presiding over the illustrious beach of the same name, the Copacabana sits with its grandiose art deco architecture on the doorstep of one of the world's party hot spots. Unsurprisingly it's always pulled in the rich and famous – Fred Astaire and Ginger Rogers have danced here and the Stones hung out in the bar before their famed beach concert in 2006. Other notable guests have included Brazilian supermodel Gisele Bündchen, Hollywood power couple Tom Cruise and Katie Holmes, Madonna, Michael Jackson and Luciano Pavarotti

Copacabana and Ipanema dominate the beach headlines in Rio, but larger than either is Barra de Tijuca, in the city's southwest.

✪ SUNSET MARQUIS HOTEL & VILLAS, LOS ANGELES, USA

Yep, they're all here, have been at some point, or doubtless will be again: Bono, Brittney Spears, Brad Pitt and Courtney Love (who sung about it)...the list goes on. And there's no shortage of celebrity deals being done in the complex's Bar 1200, the best bet for spotting stars and stars-in-the-making. The Sunset Marquis

ANGELO CAVALLI » PHOTOLIBRARY

has been a magnet for A-listers (think the Stones and Marley) since opening in 1963. With a basement recording studio, it's seen its fair share of riotous parties and gigs studded by famous names, but works as an oasis of calm in a frenetic part of LA, too, offering secluded villas just moments from the nearby Sunset Strip razzmatazz.

Want to see where the stars actually live? Hollywood tours (www.hollywoodtours.us) run trips to some 45 movie stars' homes.

✪ THE LANESBOROUGH, LONDON, ENGLAND

London's most expensive digs, boasting phenomenal views of Buckingham Palace, make even the Ritz across the park look second rate. You'll need to part with the best part of £10,000 (US$16,200) for a sleepover in the lavish Royal Suite, but money is no object to the Lanesborough's clientele, which encompasses a host of visiting heads of state, as well as celebs like Leonardo DiCaprio and Madonna. Stars particularly relish the hotel's privacy (the location of the best suites is known only to a handful of staff); laptops in every room and round-the-clock butler services are just some of the perks you'll receive for splashing your cash.

More lavishness awaits round the corner at Buckingham Palace. The State Rooms and the Queen's Gallery are open to the public (www.royalcollection.org.uk).

☻ AMBASSADOR EAST, CHICAGO, USA

During Prohibition, Chicago was the glam gangster capital of the world and the Ambassador East the epicentre. Al Capone's brother's alleged speakeasy was in the penthouse suite. The hotel has constantly reinvented itself; once alcohol was legalised again, Frank Sinatra and Judy Garland stayed and patronised its soon-legendary Pump Room bar, still decorated with famed guests. Hitchcock shot several scenes of his thriller *North by Northwest* here. The Ambassador still keeps the chic in Chicago, exuding art deco sophistication to such an extent that other boutique hotels struggle to keep pace.

Whether you wish to step into the shoes of Al Capone or Cary Grant, the Ambassador East (www.theambassadoreasthotel .com) can oblige.

☻ PARK HYATT, TOKYO, JAPAN

In a city where space is at a premium, the Hyatt's 50-sq-metre rooms make it a natural celebrity choice. Most recognisable to the common people as the hotel haunted by Bill Murray and Scarlett Johansson in Sofia Coppola's *Lost in Translation,* it offers a bird's-eye view (quite literally) of Mount Fuji from its 52nd-storey top floor. Ultra-modern it may be, but there are plenty of traditional Japanese touches, like ancient Hokkaido water elm panelling in the rooms. The likes of Nicole Kidman and Mariah Carey have graced the guest list.

If your budget doesn't stretch to a stay, try dining (still steep) in the hotel's stylish New York Bar (www.tokyo.park.hyatt .com): it has amazing views of Tokyo.

☻ THE CARLYLE, NEW YORK, USA

The Waldorf-Astoria might have the edge on antique decor and the Soho Grand might resonate more contemporary cool but the Carlyle is a discerning celebrity favourite, and offers more room size for your money. Mick Jagger and Jack Nicholson regularly stay; JFK even had a permanent suite here. Its eye-catching exterior and location on Madison Ave draw you in to an elegant interior dating back to its 1930 inception, with modern twists designed by the likes of Thierry Despont.

Woody Allen's most regular New York gigs take place in the Carlyle with the Eddy Davis New Orleans Jazz Band, on Mondays at 8.45pm.

☻ PALMS CASINO RESORT, LAS VEGAS, USA

This mammoth complex sports the world's only hotel basketball court and Playboy club, along with its own rock 'n' roll venue and a recording studio. But the Palms is also unusual in being simultaneously *the* celebrity check-in choice in Vegas and comparatively affordable, both for its renowned nightlife (still pretty much the city's best) and for its rooms. Of course the celebrity suites don't come in the affordable category: themed around everything from bowling lanes to Hollywood directors, these elegies in extravagance could set you back tens of thousands of dollars.

If you're in town to gamble, try the ultra-opulent Bellagio (www.bellagio.com) or Luxor (www.luxor.com), modelled on an Egyptian pyramid.

INDEX

ACKNOWLEDGEMENTS

PUBLISHER Piers Pickard

ASSOCIATE PUBLISHER Ben Handicott

COMMISSIONING EDITOR & PROJECT MANAGER Bridget Blair

DESIGNERS Christopher Ong, Seviora Citra, James Hardy

LAYOUT DESIGNER Nicholas Colicchia, Jessica Rose

EDITORS Peter Cruttenden, Jackey Coyle, Pat Kinsella

IMAGE RESEARCHERS Rebecca Skinner, Aude Vauconsant

PRE-PRESS PRODUCTION Ryan Evans

PRINT PRODUCTION Yvonne Kirk

WRITTEN BY Sarah Baxter, Michael Benanav, Stuart Butler, Jean-Bernard Carrillet, Piera Chen, Kerry Christiani, Gregor Clark, Tom Hall, Abigail Hole, Robert Kelly, Jessica Lee, Shawn Low, Anirban Mahapatra, Carolyn McCarthy, Craig McLachlan, Anja Mutic, Sally O'Brien, Robert Reid, Dan Savery Raz, Oliver Smith, Luke Waterson, Meg Worby, Karla Zimmerman

THANKS TO Heather Dickson, Imogen Hall, Nic Lehman, Kylie McLaughlin, Tasmin McNaughtan, Kate Morgan, Mazzy Prinsep, Marg Toohey, Tony Wheeler

LONELY PLANET'S BEST IN TRAVEL 2012
October 2011

ISBN 978 1 74220 305 8

PUBLISHED BY
Lonely Planet Publications Pty Ltd
ABN 36 005 607 983
90 Maribyrnong St, Footscray,
Victoria, 3011, Australia

www.lonelyplanet.com

Printed in Singapore

10 9 8 7 6 5 4 3 2 1

Lonely Planet's preferred image source is Lonely Planet Images (LPI).
www.lonelyplanetimages.com

LONELY PLANET OFFICES

AUSTRALIA Locked Bag 1, Footscray, Victoria, 3011
Phone 03 8379 8000 Fax 03 8379 8111
Email talk2us@lonelyplanet.com.au
USA 150 Linden St, Oakland, CA 94607
Phone 510 250 6400 Toll free 800 275 8555
Fax 510 893 8572
Email info@lonelyplanet.com
UK 2nd Floor, 186 City Rd, London, ECV1 2NT
Phone 020 7106 2100 Fax 020 7106 2101
Email go@lonelyplanet.co.uk

FRONT COVER IMAGE London - Derek Croucher/Photolibrary **INSIDE BACK COVER IMAGE** Hong Kong - James Marshall/LPI

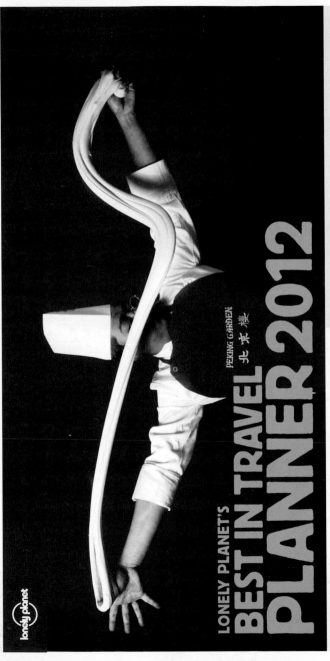

LONELY PLANET'S
BEST IN TRAVEL
PLANNER 2012

PEKING GARDEN 北京燥

JANUARY

MUSCAT FESTIVAL » OMAN
An extravaganza - everything from cuisine and handicraft demos to fashion parades, mainly set against the lush backdrop of Qurum National Park (p100).

SANTIAGO A MIL » CHILE
Latin America's biggest theatre festival, Santiago a Mil (loosely translated as Santiago Rush) brings drama from cultural centres to the street, with international works, emerging theatre and acrobats (p121).

TORGYA & LOSAR FESTIVALS » INDIA
Features masked Tibetan Buddhist dances in one of the world's biggest Buddhist monasteries, Tawang in Arunachal Pradesh (p66).

FEBRUARY

CARNEVALE » ITALY
The baroque coastal resort of Acireale, Sicily, comes alive with gargantuan papier mâché puppets, flowery allegorical floats, confetti and fireworks (p74).

LANTERN FESTIVAL » TAIWAN
Celebrations include dazzling laser shows and mass releases of paper sky lanterns, drawing in the crowds two weeks after Lunar New Year. The main 2012 events will be held in historic Lukang town (p44).

FASNACHT » SWITZERLAND
A must-see carnival in Basel, with its torchlit processions, spectacular costumed parades, fifers and drummers (p48).

lonely planet